HORRIBLE SCIENCE

MICROSCOPIC MONSTERS AND DEADLY DISEASES

Two Horrible Books in One

NICK ARNOLD
TONY DE SAULLES

D1340204

■SCHOLASTIC

Scholastic Children's Books,
Commonwealth House, 1-19 New Oxford Street,
London WC1A 1NU, UK

A division of Scholastic Ltd
London ~ New York ~ Toronto ~ Sydney ~ Auckland
Mexico City ~ New Delhi ~ Hong Kong

Published in this edition by Scholastic Ltd, 2004
Cover illustration copyright © Tony De Saulles, 2004

Microscopic Monsters
First published in the UK by Scholastic Ltd, 2001
Text copyright © Nick Arnold, 2001
Illustrations copyright © Tony De Saulles, 2001

Deadly Diseases
First published in the UK by Scholastic Ltd, 2000
Text copyright © Nick Arnold, 2000
Illustrations copyright © Tony De Saulles, 2000

ISBN 0 439 97316 3

Typeset by M Rules
Printed and bound by AIT Nørhaven A/S, Denmark

10 9 8 7 6 5 4 3 2

The right of Nick Arnold and Tony De Saulles to be identified as the author and
illustrator of this work respectively has been asserted by them in accordance
with the Copyright, Designs and Patents Act, 1988.

Contents

MICROSCOPIC MONSTERS

Nick Arnold has been writing stories and books since he was a youngster, but never dreamt he'd find fame writing about Horrible Science. His research involved interviewing fleas and trying out plague cures and he enjoyed every minute of it.

When he's not delving into Horrible Science, he spends his spare time eating pizza, riding his bike and thinking up corny jokes (though not all at the same time).

Tony De Saulles picked up his crayons when he was still in nappies and has been doodling ever since. He takes Horrible Science very seriously and even agreed to draw magnified toilet germs and cholera-carrying mosquitoes. Fortunately, he has made a full recovery.

When he's not out with his sketchpad, Tony likes to write poetry and play squash, though he hasn't written any poetry about squash yet.

INTRODUCTION

Which of these is the smallest?

a) Your pocket money.

MISERLY AMOUNT

b) Your teacher's brain.

PATHETICALLY PUNY

c) A mite (a bug that looks like a scaled-down spider).

TINY BUT TERRIFYING

Well, hopefully you said **c)** because at just 0.2 mm (0.008 inches), a mite is one of the smallest objects anyone can see. Your eyes can't see smaller things because the lenses in your eyeballs can't focus on them. And that means that whatever you look at has a whole lot of detail that's too small to make out. This tiny world can be very incredible, and very beautiful (they say small is beautiful don't they?).

But it can also be very *horrible*!

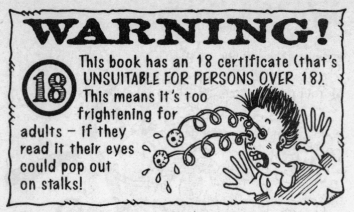

WARNING!

18 This book has an 18 certificate (that's UNSUITABLE FOR PERSONS OVER 18). This means it's too frightening for adults – if they read it their eyes could pop out on stalks!

Now, as I said, your eyes can't see tiny things, but your mind's eye can *imagine* them. And when you read this book your imagination will be working so hard there'll be steam coming out your ears! You'll be imagining a whole new world – the terribly tiny microscopic world. And as you're about to find out, it's a world of violence and sudden death.

Yes, it's a world of microscopic horrors and MONSTERS that make made-up monsters in stories appear loveable and fluffy. And make no mistake – the microscopic monsters in this book are as REAL as you are! At this very second they're strolling on your skin and snuggling into your bed and scoffing your sandwiches and splashing about in your toilet! So brace yourself for a feast of fearsomely fascinating facts. Find out…

• how millions of creatures *die* when you walk on the grass.

- what slimy animals lurk between your *teeth*.

- how germs can make dead bodies *explode*.

- and WORST OF ALL, how flushing the toilet can cover you in *poo*.

No, you'd best read this book right now before someone else takes it away and starts reading it for themselves!

9

MAGICAL MICROSCOPES

COOL!

You might be surprised to learn that this book is more than just a book ... IT'S A MICROSCOPE!

The magic microscope

You're holding a *microscope* ... a wonderful instrument for peering at tiny objects and seeing them like no human eye ever can. A device for making things appear hundreds of times larger than they really are...

YEAH, RIGHT!

What's that? This book doesn't look like a microscope? Oh, but I'm telling you it *is* – try putting your eye up close to this circle. Look closely...

Concentrate hard ... very hard ... see anything?

NO!

Well, look over the page and prepare to be amazed. Thanks to the power of this book ... er, I mean microscope, we are now looking at the page enlarged 100 times.

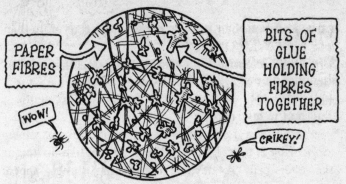

PAPER FIBRES

BITS OF GLUE HOLDING FIBRES TOGETHER

WOW!

CRIKEY!

So you knew that paper is made up of little fibres that were once wood from trees? Well, here's your chance to check out what else you know...

A tiny, tiny quiz
This quiz is so easy that you're even told what the answers are! Trouble is, the letters in the answers are muddled up so you've got to work out what they say!

1 Whenever you ride your bike the tyres leave tiny microscopic traces of melted ... REBRUB.
2 A fungus makes microscopic seeds called spores. When the sun shines they go dark just like you do when you get a ... STUNNA.
3 When you go outside your hair, your clothes and the snot in your nose become coated in thousands of microscopic bits of rock half the width of a hair. They're known as ... TRIG.
4 At the heart of every raindrop is a microscopic speck of dust. Some of this dust fell to Earth from ... ROUTE CAPES.
5 Look at a spider's web under a microscope and you'll see tiny lumps of ... GUEL.
6 All the tiny bits of dirt and dead skin that you've

washed off your hair in your life would weigh more than your ... HOWLE ODBY.

7 In 1848 scientist John Queckett peered through his microscope at a scrap of leather that had been nailed to a church door. He was shocked to discover it was really ... UNHAM INKS.

UNHAM INKS! THAT'S DISGUSTING!

Answers:

1 No, not *rhubarb* – it's RUBBER. When your tyres touch the road a tiny surface layer 0.025 mm (0.001 inches) thick melts – so in fact your wheel slides over the ground! The tyre cools immediately as the wheel turns away from the road but microscopic traces of rubber remain stuck to the tarmac. When your tyre has lost lots of rubber it looks worn and tyred. I mean tired.

2 Are you stunned? It's a SUNTAN. Yes, fungal spores get suntans and the chemical that makes this dark colour is melanin – the same substance that makes the dark colour in human skin!

3 Yes, it's a TRICY question. It's GRIT, made up of finely ground-up rock or sand just 0.03 mm (0.0012 inches) in size that's blown on the wind. Some grit comes from deserts or erupting volcanoes on the other side of the world! If it gets in your pudding you could have a bit of desert in your dessert!

4 Every day millions of specks of dust about 0.002 mm (0.00008 inches) across fall to Earth from OUTER SPACE. Inside a cloud drops of rain form around the dust and when a raindrop plops down the back of your neck you could be making contact with a 4.7 billion-year-old lump of alien rock! It's even older than your dad's favourite music – that's just ancient rock.

5 Do they serve GUEL in your school dinners? Actually, it's GLUE to stick insects to the web. Did you know that spider's silk is one of the strongest materials in the world – yet a spider's web that stretched around the world would weigh no more than an orange?

6 Don't "HOWL ODDLY" – it's WHOLE BODY! In just one year you could collect 3 kg (6.61 lbs) of grotty, greasy gunk from your hair. You could fill a small bucket and butter your sandwiches with it!

7 What do you INK this stuff is? It turned out to be HUMAN SKIN cut from a dead Viking 900 years before. Well, I'm sure the Viking was really cut up about that.

So how did you get on? If you thought it was easy then maybe you fancy really getting to grips with the microscopic world.

Test your teacher...

WHO INVENTED THE MICROSCOPE?

Answer: The correct answer is "I dunno!" because no one is sure – but teachers don't like admitting they don't know things and historians don't mind guessing...

The truth is, ALL three *said* they invented the microscope. Well, I suppose anyone could have made the discovery. Once you've got a couple of lenses (the glass bits that make objects appear larger) it's easy enough to put them together and realize that two lenses make things appear larger than just one lens. And when your arms start aching from holding the lenses apart at the right distance to see tiny things in focus, sooner or later you'll hit on the idea of sticking the lenses at either end of a tube. And hey presto – you've invented the microscope!

But what about the lens? Well, guess what – no one's too sure who invented the lens either! We've brought some experts together to try and solve the mystery.

1 Archaeologists have found a piece of rock crystal in a cave on the island of Crete. It was carved 4,500 years ago.

IT'S SHAPED LIKE A LENS AND IT MAKES THINGS LOOK BIGGER!

2 In 1850 archaeologists found another lens-shaped crystal in what is now Iraq. It was carved by the Assyrian people in 800 BC.

MINE'S BETTER QUALITY – IT'S CRYSTAL CLEAR!

YES, BUT MINE'S OLDER!

3 Boring historians point out that there is no actual *proof* that these crystals were used as lenses at all. But there is proof in the writings of short-sighted Roman philosopher Seneca (AD 4-65) that he used a bowl of water as a lens to help him read the scrolls at his local library. So does that mean Seneca invented the lens?

IT'S TRANSPARENTLY OBVIOUS!

SOUNDS FISHY TO US!

15

Lovely lenses

Anyway, *someone* invented the lens and around 1300 someone else in Italy (yes, you guessed it, no one knows who) found out how to grind glass to make lenses. The trick was getting the right shape – wanna know how it's done? Well, why not make your own? Go on, it's easy!

Dare you discover ... how to make your own lens?

In the olden days you had to cut the glass carefully to shape and then grind it with gritty substances by hand until you had made exactly the right curve. And then you had to "polish" it to get rid of any scratches. (Basically, this meant grinding the glass some more with fine powders.) This grinding might take days of toil.

But you'll be pleased to know there's an easier way...

What you need:
A bottle shaped like this…
(An empty mouthwash bottle is ideal.)

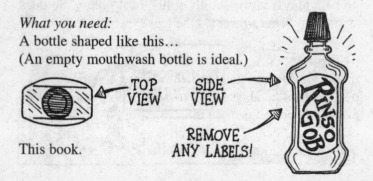

16

What you do:

1 Completely fill the bottle with water so there are no air bubbles.

2 Place the bottle sideways on over this page, put your eye close to the bottle and look at this fascinating blood-sucking flea.

HURRY UP,
I HAVEN'T
GOT ALL DAY!

You should be able to see that the flea has got bigger – but how? Here's a clue: you have to imagine light bouncing off the page and bouncing into your eyeballs.

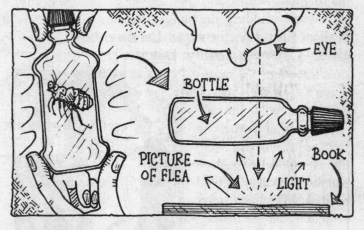

Which of these explanations is correct:

a) The light speeds up as it passes through water and this makes your brain think the flea is bigger than it is.

b) The water bends the light towards a point. If I put my eye at this point I can see the flea close up.

c) The water makes the light brighter and this makes my brain think that the flea is bigger.

For about 70 years after they were invented, microscopes weren't terribly powerful and few scientists had cottoned on to the potential of the new invention. But a lone genius was about to change all that. With his own hands he would make the most powerful microscopes then known and use them to make some monster discoveries...

Hall of fame: Antony van Leeuwenhoek
(1632-1723) Nationality: Dutch

Leeuwenhoek means "Lion's Corner" – which was the name of the café Antony's dad owned in Delft, Holland. Oh well, things could have been worse. Antony could have been named after something on the menu – he might have had to go through life as "Antony Supa-dupa whopper-burger"!

EGG AND CHIPS READY FOR TABLE NINE!

Antony's dad died when he was still at school. The young boy went to live with a relative and learnt how to be a cloth merchant. For much of his life he was a quietly

18

hard-working, quietly prosperous shopkeeper in his home town of Delft. It sounds seriously boring but at least he had an interesting hobby...

You've guessed it! Microscopes!

Like other cloth sellers of the time, Antony used a lens to check the quality of his wares by checking the condition of the threads that made up the cloth. But unlike the others, Antony was *seriously* into lenses. He actually enjoyed grinding and polishing them laboriously by hand, and he mounted them on metal plates to make simple microscopes. Here's one now...

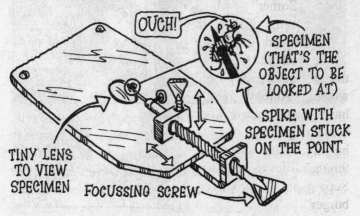

Antony was very good at his work because he had incredibly sharp eyesight which was ideal for spotting tiny details and he was a very curious man – I mean curious in the sense of wanting to find out more about the tiny world. So he decided to use his microscope to look at other tiny things. One day he looked at a raindrop and saw that it was alive with tiny slithering creatures. Encouraged, he checked his own spit, skin, tree bark, leaves and one of his rotten teeth after someone pulled it out. And everywhere he saw tiny wriggling creatures. He was the first human being to glimpse the things that we now call bacteria (for the slimy details see page 70).

Before Leeuwenhoek, people had no idea that things could happen on a scale too small for them to see. So they made up fanciful explanations for why things happen...

But Leeuwenhoek saw flea eggs through his microscope, and realized that's where fleas came from. (So it sounds like his work was up to scratch!) Then he looked at tiny baby eels, and proved that people were wrong when they said that eels formed from dew. Yes, once again he dew the right conclusion! Leeuwenhoek was so keen on his microscopes that he nearly blinded himself watching gunpowder explode at close quarters. And that nearly blew his chances of seeing anything!

As Antony's excitement grew he wrote letters to the Royal Society, the top scientific club in Britain, and told them about his discoveries. Here's what one letter might have said (the letter was in Dutch but we've translated it)...

To Henry Oldenberg,
Secretary of
the Royal Society

SHOP AT
LEEUWENHOEK'S
CLOTH SHOP!

No job too small!
Delft, Holland

September 1676

Dear Henry

You'll never guess what I've found! I was out for a stroll by a swampy lake called Berkelse Mere. The lake's all green and smelly. Local people think the colour comes from dew. Well, I thought, it might be interesting to check out the water with the help of my brilliant microscope. And as luck would have it, I had a glass specimen tube with me - I never leave home without one!

   Into the lake I splashed! My knickerbockers were ruined, I'll never get the smelly slime stains off - but it was worth it! Under the microscope I saw that the green colour

21

was actually tiny little strands, thinner than a hair. And there were things like tiny green raspberries swimming about and little creatures shaped like blobs of jelly squishing around. Well, my legs turned to jelly too. At this point, I realized I was looking at life forms unknown to science! Is this great or what? →

Yours, Tony

The Royal Society, London.

October 1676

Dear Antony

We've had a chat about your letter and we reckon you're telling whopping porkie-pies. In other words, we think you're fibbing! Little creatures in water? Yeah - right, pull the other one! You'll be telling us that these creatures cause disease next!

Let's see you prove it - OK!?

Yours crossly,
Henry Oldenberg →

A QUICK NOTE...

Antony got some important people to write saying that they'd seen the little creatures too. The creatures really did exist and today we know they were tiny plants called algae and microscopic life forms known as protozoa (pro-toe-zo-a).

Leeuwenhoek published a book on his work and became famous. Soon scientific clubs were rushing to have him as a member and kings and lords flocked to his little shop and begged to look at germs. Leeuwenhoek died at the ripe old age of 90 with his eyesight still perfect, and as a parting gift he left some microscopes to his old pals at the Royal Society. Each had a tiny lump of dried blood or hair or teeth or muscle glued to the spike. Unfortunately, the glue rotted and the tiny specimens fell off.

Leeuwenhoek's microscopes really were the business – some could make out things 0.0015 mm (0.0006 inches) across! But no one knew how he could grind such incredible lenses and he never shared his skills with anyone. He feared people might copy him. So could YOU follow in Leeuwenhoek's footsteps and become a great microscope scientist? To help you here's ... the world's smallest ruler...

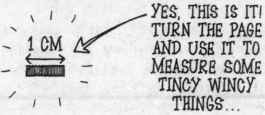

1 CM

YES, THIS IS IT! TURN THE PAGE AND USE IT TO MEASURE SOME TINCY WINCY THINGS...

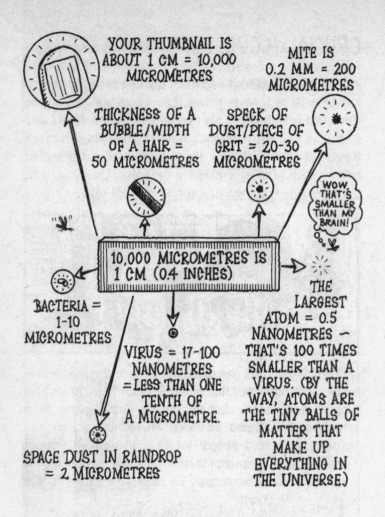

YOUR THUMBNAIL IS ABOUT 1 CM = 10,000 MICROMETRES

MITE IS 0.2 MM = 200 MICROMETRES

THICKNESS OF A BUBBLE/WIDTH OF A HAIR = 50 MICROMETRES

SPECK OF DUST/PIECE OF GRIT = 20-30 MICROMETRES

WOW, THAT'S SMALLER THAN MY BRAIN!

10,000 MICROMETRES IS 1 CM (0.4 INCHES)

BACTERIA = 1-10 MICROMETRES

VIRUS = 17-100 NANOMETRES = LESS THAN ONE TENTH OF A MICROMETRE.

THE LARGEST ATOM = 0.5 NANOMETRES — THAT'S 100 TIMES SMALLER THAN A VIRUS. (BY THE WAY, ATOMS ARE THE TINY BALLS OF MATTER THAT MAKE UP EVERYTHING IN THE UNIVERSE.)

SPACE DUST IN RAINDROP = 2 MICROMETRES

Got your head round all that? Great! But getting to grips with a microscope is no small task. You're going to need a bit more knowhow and, oddly enough, that's what you're going to pick up in the next chapter...

CRUCIAL MICROSCOPIC {KNOWHOW}

In this chapter you can practise using a microscope and even follow in Leeuwenhoek's footsteps and make your own. But first, a quick jog down memory lane to the bad old days of microscopes. The days when your science teacher strutted around in a powdered wig and an embarrassing floppy cravat.

THE NEW BLURMORE
~ (1730 MODEL) ~
MICROSCOPE

INSTRUCTIONS
Congratulations on buying the Blurmore microscope. It's the hi-tech way to see very small things that we scientists don't really understand yet! Here's how to examine a slug...

1 Kill the slug and dry its body. Then soak it in blood. The blood will dry and harden around the slug. This way it's easy to cut its body into thin slices with a sharp knife to study its slimy innards.

2 Lay a slice of slug on a microscope slide. Add a few blobs of smelly glue made of boiled up fish-bones to hold your slug in position. If you happen to be out of fish you could try a blob of fat from a dead animal.

GAZOOKS!

3 Now you are ready to look at your slide, so simply place it under the lens of your microscope and peer through the eyepiece!

~ **THE SMALL PRINT** ~

1. Our lenses are rather blurry and colours appear in the glass like a rainbow and that makes it a bit confusing. But hey — it's pretty!

2. Your slide will quickly rot and become smelly.

Things could only get better...

1 In 1830 microscope enthusiast Joseph Lister (1786-1869) designed a new type of microscope. It had two lenses fitted together and each lens was made out of a different type of glass. For complex reasons to do with the way light bends through the different types of glass, this cut out the confusing colours.

2 Also in the 1830s you could buy pure glass lenses that were clearer than the old types of glass which had traces of other chemicals that made them blurry. You could say the new lenses were clearly better!

3 Remember how you had to cut the specimen into thin slices? By the 1860s scientists had learnt how to cover the specimen in paraffin wax to hold it steady before they cut it. The idea made slicing easier and safer so I guess it proved a cut above the rest.

4 By the 1890s scientists were using a chemical called formalin to harden the specimen before the wax stage. The formalin preserved the specimen and made it easier to cut. The discovery was made by a scientist who was using formalin to kill germs on a dead mouse. But he absent-mindedly left the mouse in the formalin overnight and in the morning it was harder than a school cheese.

Today undertakers use formalin to preserve dead bodies but school cheeses are preserved using slightly less poisonous chemicals.

Still want to be a microscope expert?
Wow, that's great! This magazine should be right up your eyepiece...

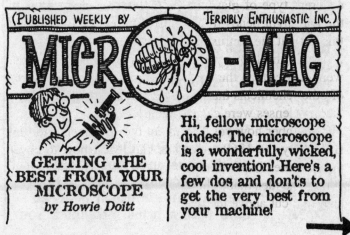

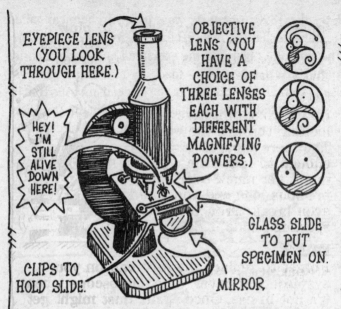

EYEPIECE LENS (YOU LOOK THROUGH HERE.)

OBJECTIVE LENS (YOU HAVE A CHOICE OF THREE LENSES EACH WITH DIFFERENT MAGNIFYING POWERS.)

HEY! I'M STILL ALIVE DOWN HERE!

GLASS SLIDE TO PUT SPECIMEN ON.

CLIPS TO HOLD SLIDE.

MIRROR

DOS AND DON'TS

DO

Shine a bright light on your microscope. The mirror will reflect light under the specimen. Of course, if the object is solid like the head of a dead insect you could try lighting the object from above otherwise it'll appear as a dark blob and you blobably won't see much.

1

2

ERK!

DO

Use a very soft cloth or air brush to remove dust from your microscope lenses. (Oh, by the way, an air brush is an air bulb with a brush attached. You squeeze the bulb and puff air to blow away that nasty dust and the brush gets rid of any sticky bits.) TLC for lenses – that's what I say!

DON'T
Lower your objective whilst looking through the eyepiece. The mere thought of this is enough to make me cry! You might get muck over your precious lens and you could even break through your glass specimen slide – BOO HOO!

CRACK!

DON'T
Forget to replace the dust cap on your eyepiece and cover your microscope when it's not in use. Once again, dust might get on the lenses. And then all your observations could bite the dust...

MIND YOU, DUST CAN BE FASCINATING – JUST TURN TO PAGE 86 IF YOU DON'T BELIEVE ME!

JUST TURN TO PAGE 86 IF YOU DON'T BELIEVE ME!

Microscopic expressions

Two microscope scientists are talking...

WAS THE DEPTH OF FIELD OK FOR THE BODY TUBE?

YES – BUT I LACKED THE RESOLUTION!

Do you say...?

> HELP! THEY'VE MURDERED SOMEONE AND PUT THE BODY IN A TUBE AND THEN BURIED IT IN A FIELD AND ONE OF THEM IS FEELING SCARED!

Answer: Poppycock, codswallop, humbug! The body tube is the main part of a microscope that contains the lenses. Depth of field means the amount that you can move the body tube up and down and still get a clear image and resolution means the amount of detail you can see. D'you see?

Bet you never knew!
How scientists make slides of specimens...
1 They stain the specimen so it shows up really clearly under the microscope. A stain is a special dye that colours certain chemicals and shows up certain parts of the tiny object the scientist is looking at. A commonly used stain is cochineal – made from ground up beetles!

GULP!

NEXT!

2 Cut a thin slice of the object. That's so that the light can shine through it from below and you can see it clearly under the microscope. How thin? Well about one thousandth of a millimetre (one micrometre) will do. Scientists use a tool called a microtome to do the cutting – and I expect very mean scientists use it to cut cake.

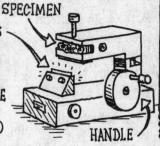

SPECIMEN

THE BLADE IS MADE FROM VERY SHARP GLASS (ITS CUTTING EDGE IS SHARPER THAN METAL)

RIGHT, THAT'S ONE MICROMETRE FOR YOU AND THE REST FOR ME!

HANDLE

3 *They place the specimen on a glass with a drop of water to stop it drying out and a thin piece of glass called a cover slip to protect it. Or if they want to store the specimen they might cover it in glycerine and gelatine and seal the edges of the cover slip with gum arabic to stop it from drying or rotting.*

☠ HORRIBLE HEALTH WARNING!

Don't you try cutting *your* specimens! You might end up examining an interesting slice of fingertip!

Now as I said, this book is a *microscope*. And you don't need another microscope to read this book. (Unless you're *really* short-sighted!) But if you'd like another microscope, here's how to make one so powerful that everyone in your class will be jealous including your teacher! Think about it ... your very own ELECTRON MICROSCOPE!

Microscopic monsters fact file

NAME: Electron microscope

THE BASIC FACTS: **1** An electron microscope fires electrons at the object you're looking at. (Electrons are the tiny blips of energy that surround atoms.)

2 Like electrons, light is made of tiny blips of energy but they zig-zag very fast to form light waves. If the object is smaller than a light wave (0.5 micrometres) then your eyes won't be able to see it *with an ordinary microscope.*

VIEWING SCREEN   COMPUTER

3 The beam of electrons is far smaller than a light wave. So you can actually study objects 200,000 times smaller than with an ordinary microscope.

BEE'S KNEES

DEADLY VIRUS

MONSTROUS DETAILS: An electron microscope is fab for looking at really horrible tiny objects. Things like the viruses that cause deadly diseases such as rabies.

How to build your own scanning electron microscope

Wanna get closer to the action? Well, if your answer is "Not 'arf" then you've come to the right place!

First assemble your materials...

A large metal pipe. (A sewer pipe will do – better give it a good scrub!)

A fluorescent screen and electron gun from a TV set. (No, don't take your TV set to pieces, I'm sure you can borrow one from school.)

Some *very* powerful magnets.

A computer. (It needs software suitable for presenting pictures from an electron microscope. Perhaps a friendly computer programmer could knock you up some?)

A powerful air pump to suck air out of the microscope and form an airless space called a vacuum.

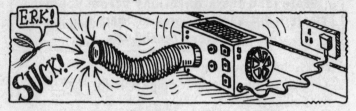

A wire and plug linked up to the electron gun.

Here's what you do...

1 Fix the electrode gun in the metal pipe so that it fires a beam of high energy electrons downwards and sweeps from side to side.

2 Below this, fix magnets on either side of the pipe. The magnetic forces direct the electrons into a narrow beam. Make sure the electron beam hits the place where the specimen is to be fixed and bounces on to the fluorescent screen. The screen should light up where it's hit by electrons.

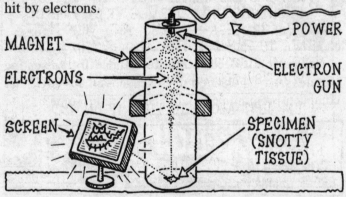

3 Link the screen up to a computer that can interpret the hits on the screen as a picture of the specimen you'll be studying.

4 Use the pump to pump out the air from the tube. Atoms of air get in the way of the electrons and distort the picture.

5 Whoops! Silly me! Don't forget to place your specimen inside the machine. Actually this should be step **4** because if you put your hand in the airless tube your fingers could be wrenched out of their sockets!

6 Plug in and switch on! NO, DON'T!!!!!!

An important announcement...

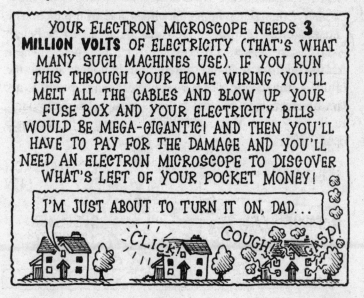

YOUR ELECTRON MICROSCOPE NEEDS **3 MILLION VOLTS** OF ELECTRICITY (THAT'S WHAT MANY SUCH MACHINES USE). IF YOU RUN THIS THROUGH YOUR HOME WIRING YOU'LL MELT ALL THE CABLES AND BLOW UP YOUR FUSE BOX AND YOUR ELECTRICITY BILLS WOULD BE MEGA-GIGANTIC! AND THEN YOU'LL HAVE TO PAY FOR THE DAMAGE AND YOU'LL NEED AN ELECTRON MICROSCOPE TO DISCOVER WHAT'S LEFT OF YOUR POCKET MONEY!

I'M JUST ABOUT TO TURN IT ON, DAD...

CLICK! COUGH GASP!

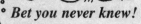

1 Electron microscopes can create images of atoms. A scanning tunnelling electron microscope is a type of electron microscope that uses a tiny probe that fires electrons at the surface of an object. It has a device to pick up the electrons as they rebound to reveal the shapes of atoms.

2 The first scanning tunnelling electron microscope was built in 1981 by Swiss scientists Gerd Binnig and Heinrich Rohrer. Their first picture showed gold atoms that looked like an upside-down cardboard egg box.

GOLD ATOMS

UPSIDE-DOWN EGG BOX

The scientists were awarded gold medals and the Nobel Prize (let's hope the medals didn't look like cardboard).

Meanwhile, back at the drawing board – here's how to build a microscope that's not quite so powerful as the electron microscope but it's easier to make and really very nice. You can use it to study this fascinating dead spider...

FASCINATING DEAD SPIDER

Dare you discover ... how to build your own microscope?

What you need:

A piece of card 2.5 cm (1 inch) wide by 5 cm (2 inches) long.

A piece of cellophane (try using the clear wrapping from a greetings card).

Scissors

Sticky tape

Pencil or hole punch.

A cardboard tube from a kitchen roll.

What you do:

1 Use the hole punch or pencil point to make a hole 5 mm (0.2 inches) across in the centre of the card.

2 Cover the hole with cellophane and secure with sticky tape.

3 Cut a length of tube 5 cm (2 inches) long and then cut into it two slots 3 cm long and 2.5 cm apart coming down from one end. Lift up the cardboard between them to make a little window. Place the tube on top of the spider and place the card on top of the tube.

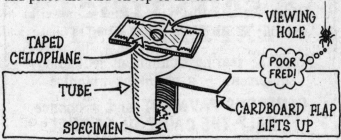

TAPED CELLOPHANE

VIEWING HOLE

POOR FRED!

TUBE

CARDBOARD FLAP LIFTS UP

SPECIMEN

4 Pick up a drop of water on the tip of the pencil and let it fall over the cellophane covering the hole. Make sure the drop covers the hole.

5 Hold your eye very close to the drop and look through it. You should see the spider's eight eyes and fangs in fascinating close up detail. Just don't let it give you nightmares afterwards...

Now just imagine you could use your microscope to spot a tiny human being. That's right an actual human being shrunk to a microscopic size. Impossible? Wait till you read this story...

It's a small world!

No one knew what to expect from the professor's new shrinking machine, but one thing was clear. The person who agreed to test it had to be ever so brave ... or ever so stupid. Only fearless private eye MI Gutzache had the experience for the job – and a very bad experience it was. And *no way* was he falling for that "all for the cause of science" cockamamie clap-trap!

But then a couple of words caught his eye...

I wasn't going to volunteer for nothing but I needed the green backs. I figured I'd done it all and seen it all – but I hadn't seen nothing. I took the case and I should have known better. It was my first mistake.

I'm afraid none of my scientific colleagues wanted to volunteer for the test - they all muttered something about "unacceptable risk factors". I explained to Gutzache that the new machine was capable of shrinking a human to the size of a microbe!

SO YOU WON'T BE NEEDING THAT!

I heard the Prof but I didn't like what I was hearing. I wanted out but the Prof suggested a small test. "No risk," he said. But he was wrong and I was the fall guy. I stood under the machine as he switched it on. Just one tiny little test...

I placed a pin upright under the microscope but outside the shrinking ray for Gutzache to inspect and report on. It would be a fascinating opportunity to compare Gutzache's view with that of the microscope.

Gutzache felt the gentle warmth of the rays falling on him like summer sunshine. It didn't feel too bad until he noticed that he was shrinking. The pin beside him was getting bigger and bigger until it looked like a giant column. There were ridges and furrows running down its sides and its top was no longer sharp and pointed but rounded like an enormous Christmas pudding.

The big, wide world was getting bigger and wider by the second. Too big. A good private eye plays a hunch and mine said "get out!" - but it was too late. The pin wasn't a pin - it looked like the Washington Monument. And that wasn't all. There were things squirming and oozing in the wrinkles that appeared in the metal. Living things - like squelching blobs of jelly. The pin didn't look too lucky and I was hollering for the Prof to make me bigger.

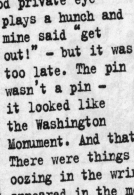

WASHINGTON MONUMENT

41

Amazing! Gutzache is describing microscopic dents and bacteria on the pin. At this point I observed Gutzache under the microscope. I could see him waving even if I couldn't hear his tiny voice. He seemed happy so I decided to press on. But just then I had ... ahem, an unfortunate accident... Well, I sneezed...

It was like something blew up somewhere close. It blew me off my feet and sent me flying. I saw blobs all around, I figured they were snot. Getting in the way of a sneeze is bad for you - it sure was bad for me. Didn't the Prof know about handkerchiefs?

The floor looked hundreds of miles away and the only way was down. One thing I knew for sure - thanks to a sneeze ... I was gonna be crowbait.

Will Gutzache make a tiny little mess on the carpet? You can find out later! But first we'll stick with the detective theme and find out how microscopes solve small but messy mysteries ... including the sinister case of the treacherous toilet thief!

MICROSCOPIC DETECTIVE MYSTERIES

There's a whole branch of police work called forensic science that uses microscopes to search for clues to crimes. Here are some forensic clues that we've borrowed from a police museum.

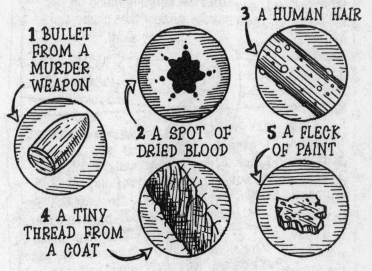

1 BULLET FROM A MURDER WEAPON

3 A HUMAN HAIR

2 A SPOT OF DRIED BLOOD

5 A FLECK OF PAINT

4 A TINY THREAD FROM A COAT

And here's how these clues can catch a villain...

Microscopic monsters fact file

NAME: Forensic science

THE BASIC FACTS: Forensic scientists check the scene of a crime for tiny clues.

THE VICTIM SEEMS TO HAVE BEEN HOLDING A BOWL OF, ER, TOMATO SOUP AT THE TIME OF THE SHOOTING...

1 Scratches on the side of the bullet might match grooves in the barrel of the suspect's gun – who said science isn't groovy?

2 Blood can be tested for DNA. This substance – known as deoxyribose nucleic acid (de-oxy-ri-bo new-clay-ick acid) – forms a unique chemical code in all of us. If DNA from the victim is found on the murder suspect then chances are they did it.

3 The hair could be matched in colour and microscopic detail to the suspect or victim.

4 The microscopic thread could be matched to a coat worn by the suspect.

5 The paint could be matched to a car driven by the suspect.

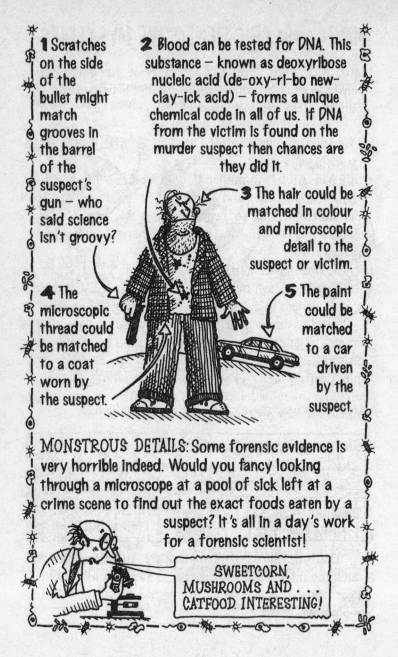

MONSTROUS DETAILS: Some forensic evidence is very horrible indeed. Would you fancy looking through a microscope at a pool of sick left at a crime scene to find out the exact foods eaten by a suspect? It's all in a day's work for a forensic scientist!

SWEETCORN, MUSHROOMS AND . . . CATFOOD. INTERESTING!

So how would you measure up as a forensic scientist? Don't worry, there won't be any pools of sick to peer into. Just a true crime story of how the microscope helped to catch a ruthless thief ... with his trousers down. Can you help trap the suspect?

The treacherous toilet thief

Lyons, France 1922

"It's a disgrace!" grumbled the old woman. "My pension money is missing and someone in your post office has stolen it! I'm 86 years old and this sort of thing didn't happen when I was a girl! There ought to be a law against it!"

The postmaster looked harassed.

"There *is* a law, madam, and rest assured I will make it my business to catch the thief and return the money."

The old woman shuffled out still wagging her skinny finger and muttering complaints. When she had gone the postmaster took a deep breath and summoned his two most trusted staff. They were very different. Jean was small and wiry and Jacques was built like an extra-large pillar box. The postmaster looked sternly at the pair.

"That's the third complaint today. I am ordering you to catch the thief before he gets us into any more trouble. I have devised a cunning plan but I am afraid it is rather unpleasant."

Jacques was so proud of winning his chief's confidence that he didn't notice the words "rather unpleasant". He beamed self-importantly.

"That's all right boss, you can count on us for anything!"

"Very well," said the postmaster. "I believe that the thief is opening the letters and stealing the money in the toilet." And with that he outlined his plan.

By the time the two postmen left they were looking rather less happy.

Jean prodded his friend's bulging tummy. "You fat fool! Why did you tell him he could count on us? Now look what you've done!"

Jacques looked as if he was going to cry. "It wasn't my fault!" he moaned. "How was I to know we'd be spying on the toilets?"

"It's a terrible inconvenience!" continued Jean.

Jacques nodded gloomily. "I know it's terrible in them conveniences, but we could always wear clothes pegs on our noses."

"Oh, shut up!" snapped Jean.

By 11 the next morning the two postmen were very uncomfortable. They were cramped and doubled up in the roof space of the toilets. And they were sickened by the revolting sights they'd been subjected to as they spied through the eyeholes that had been drilled in the ceilings of the cubicles.

"How many have you seen?" whispered Jean.

"Oh, I haven't been counting – ten, maybe 12."

"Anyone do anything bad?"

Jacques giggled. "All of them. The last one in my cubicle must have eaten lots of beans – he was a real stinker! This investigation is getting up my nose."

But Jean put his finger to his lips.

"Shut up, Jacques, there's someone in the toilet!"

"Where's he going – yours or mine?"

"Mine. Ssh, Jacques – I think it's the thief!"

There was a ripping sound as envelopes were opened and a rustling as their contents were rifled and a crackle as postal orders and bank notes were hurriedly stuffed into the thief's pockets.

"I want a look!" cried Jacques shoving aside his friend. But his huge knee banged the floor sending a fine drizzle of plaster into the cubicle. The thief hastily unlocked the door and fled the toilet.

"Now look what you've done!" hissed Jean.

"It wasn't my fault!" said Jacques miserably. "How can I help it if the floor got in the way?!"

Back in the postmaster's office the boss was drumming his fingers on the table.

"Well, what did he look like?" he asked the two postmen.

"He wore a cap," said Jacques.

The postmaster gave him a dirty look. "You fool, all postmen wear a cap – it's one of our regulations. Is that it? So all we've got is a damaged toilet roof and nothing to go on!"

Jacques whispered, "Does he mean that no one can go on the toilet?" and Jean gave him a kick.

"What was that?" said the postmaster sharply.

"Jacques said the thief might still have the envelopes on him." said Jean.

"You fool!" snapped the postmaster. "The thief is not stupid. The first thing he'll have done is to throw them away. Are you sure you didn't see anything else – any tiny clues. You'd better think of something or I'll have you watching the toilets for the next six months!"

Jean shuffled his feet unhappily. "Chief, it's not our fault! I mean – we don't have microscopes for eyes!" he said.

Suddenly the postmaster thumped his desk, making the two postmen jump.

"Microscopes!" he cried excitedly. "Of course – that's it!"

Police scientist Edmond Locard was middle-aged and neatly dressed and looked like a mild-mannered bank manager. As he listened to the postmaster's story he polished his glasses and placed the tips of his fingers together – showing off his clean, neatly trimmed fingernails.

"Hmm," he said. "A fascinating case. We'll need all the postmen's coats for microscopic laboratory analysis."

A few days later Locard was staring down the eyepiece of his microscope at the crucial evidence. His face betrayed no excitement as he adjusted the focus knob. Then he made a few neatly scripted notes in his tiny handwriting.

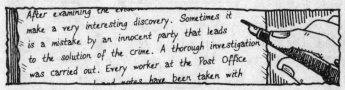

After examining the evidence... make a very interesting discovery. Sometimes it is a mistake by an innocent party that leads to the solution of the crime. A thorough investigation was carried out. Every worker at the Post Office ...and notes have been taken with

What vital clue had Locard spotted?
a) Germs that the thief picked up in the toilet.
b) Threads on the thief's coat that matched threads found in the toilet.
c) Tiny bits of plaster from the ceiling.
d) Tiny fibres of paper from the envelopes.

Answer: c) The thief had brushed his coat but there were microscopic specks of plaster still on it. If there were germs from the toilet these could have been picked up by any of the postmen, and since all the postmen wore the same type of coat the threads would not have identified the thief. Paper fibres might have proved that the thief handled the envelopes but not that he had stolen the money.

Could you be a forensic detective?

Don't worry! You *don't* have to spy on the school toilets!
Here's an easy experiment to do instead...

Dare you discover ... how to collect fibres?

What you need:
A piece of sticky tape.

What you do:
Press the sticky tape firmly on the carpet and then lift
it up.

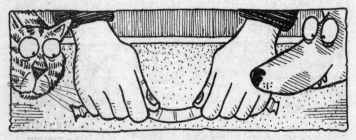

What do you notice?

Answer:
The tape is covered with carpet fibres which you can
examine with your microscope. If you're lucky, you'll
find a few human hairs or hairs from the dog or cat.
This technique is used by forensic scientists to collect
fibres from a crime scene. If they're found on the
clothes of a suspect then this could link the suspect
with the crime.

The magic microscope

Here are samples of polyester and cotton cut from two
pairs of underpants...

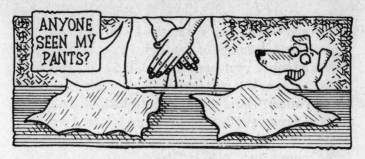

Look identical, don't they? Well, let's look closer through the magic microscope…

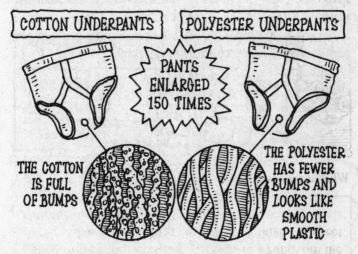

COTTON UNDERPANTS

POLYESTER UNDERPANTS

PANTS ENLARGED 150 TIMES

THE COTTON IS FULL OF BUMPS

THE POLYESTER HAS FEWER BUMPS AND LOOKS LIKE SMOOTH PLASTIC

Foul fibre facts

1 Cotton fibres come from the outer layer of seed cases on the cotton plant and they're never perfectly smooth. Polyester fibres begin life as a plastic substance that's squeezed through a tube so they're smooth and regular.

2 We've been looking at clean underwear. Seen through the microscope, dirty underwear hides all kinds of horrors. The fibres look like tangled spaghetti with lumps of brown stuff and cornflakes in it. The brown stuff is …

no, you're wrong, it's tiny bits of dirt and the "cornflakes" are lumps of dead skin.

3 Take a look at your jeans and you'll see tiny specks of white. In fact, half the threads in your blue jeans are actually white! The blue threads are dyed with indigo and if every thread was this colour the jeans would be bright blue. The white threads give the jeans a "washed 'n' faded" appearance.

4 Wool comes from sheep. Oh, so you knew that? Well, stop bleating – the fibres in wool are sheep hair and like your own hair they're made of a substance called keratin. Enlarged 1,000 times through a microscope you can see tiny scales of hair like shiny crazy paving.

Bet you never knew!
Apart from forensic scientists, there's an army of specialists who study substances such as rocks and metals in minute detail.

Now, you might think that anyone who wants to look closely at boring things like rocks and metals is the sort of person who is called Norman and wears an anorak and very thick glasses. And of course, you'd be right.

Here's Norman to explain his hobby...

The microscope is a fascinating tool for the detailed examination of substances. It can be used for the quality control of metals in factories to check for cracks between the crystals that the metals are made of.

The first scientist to study crystals in metals using a microscope was Henry Sorby (1826-1908). He sounds a bit like Norman – after all, his idea of a fun holiday was to sail his yacht up and down the coast studying how the tides move lumps of sewage that have been flushed into rivers. (He did this for a British Government Committee on the River Thames.) But he must have been a clever person because he taught himself science, and he once said his aim was...

...not to pass an examination but to qualify myself for a course for original investigation

Are you brave enough to quote this to your teacher?

In fact, microscopic investigation of materials can be very exciting – as you're about to find out...

Exciting materials quiz

Here are some exciting jobs that require a microscope. And just to make the quiz even more interesting, we've added a job for which the microscope is as sensible as a pair of exploding underpants – can you spot it?

1 Looking for the causes of a plane crash.

2 Studying rocks at the bottom of the sea.

3 Checking the quality of diamonds.

4 Looking at gold to make sure that it's 100 per cent gold and not mixed with some cheaper metal.

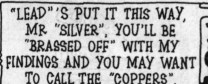

But come to think of it, there are even more scientists who use microscopes. A microscope is pretty essential for scientists who study miniature lifeforms like putrid little plants and extra small (but still revolting) bugs. They might be small, but they make up for it in the horrible habits department.

Are you ready to uncover their slimy little secrets?

Somebody had to be the first person to make an in-depth microscopic study of plants and bugs and that somebody happened to be an ugly hunch-backed dwarf. Well, that's how his friends described him ... his enemies were a little more unkind.

Hall of fame: Robert Hooke (1635-1703)
Nationality: British

Robert looked like an ugly dwarf and his hobby was spreading ugly rumours about people he didn't like such as mega-star scientist Isaac Newton (1642-1727).

NEWTON? PAH! THE MAN'S A BUFFOON. YOU'D NEED ONE OF MY MICROSCOPES TO CHECK IF HE'S GOT A BRAIN AT ALL! AND THAT RIDICULOUS FALLING APPLE THEORY, BLAH, BLAH, DRONE, WITTER, ETC. ETC.

But Hooke was also a brilliant scientist who built his own microscope and published a book called *Micrographia* full of stomach-turning pictures of his discoveries. As you might expect our old pal, Leeuwenhoek was a big fan of this book and although he couldn't read the English words he enjoyed looking at the pictures. And now for a remarkable *Horrible Science* exclusive. Here is Robert Hooke in person! He's been dug up and brought back from the dead to tell us all about his discoveries...

Dead Brainy: Robert Hooke

Is that the time? How long have I been dead?

Ah! here is my pride and joy — my microscope. Yes, you are allowed to gasp at my skill and cunning workmanship — it's all my own work you know!

OH GET ON WITH IT!

Sorry readers, RH was an extremely conceited and self-important person.

The light is provided by this oil lamp and this glass ball brightens the light and focuses it on the viewing platform on which I have placed the specimen.

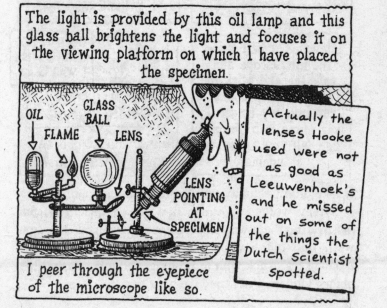

OIL
FLAME
GLASS BALL
LENS

LENS POINTING AT SPECIMEN

Actually the lenses Hooke used were not as good as Leeuwenhoek's and he missed out on some of the things the Dutch scientist spotted.

I peer through the eyepiece of the microscope like so.

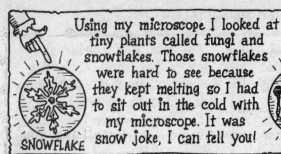

Using my microscope I looked at tiny plants called fungi and snowflakes. Those snowflakes were hard to see because they kept melting so I had to sit out in the cold with my microscope. It was snow joke, I can tell you!

SNOWFLAKE

FUNGI

One day I was looking at cork. Cork is a type of wood and I saw little boxes. Well, I called them "cells". It was a corker of a discovery — if I say so myself!

I was especially interested in plants. I looked at a stinging nettle and saw it had tiny hairs on its leaves. 'Hair's a mystery!' I thought — what are they for?

I touched a hair under the microscope and saw the end stick in my skin and poison run into my finger. I was stung into action I can tell you! Let's try it again...

OUCH — MY HAND! I WISH I WAS DEAD!

Hooke didn't actually understand what cells are for and how they worked (*you* can find out on page 103) but discovering them was still a great achievement. Later on we'll find out how Hooke studied bugs, but for the moment let's stick with those fungi and other nasty little plants. Oh yes, I'm afraid we have to...

Microscopic monsters fact file

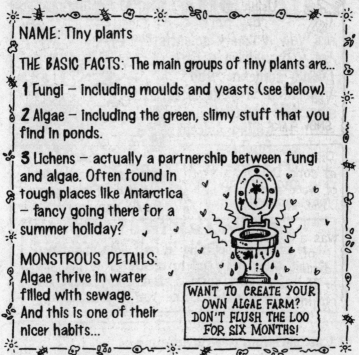

NAME: Tiny plants

THE BASIC FACTS: The main groups of tiny plants are...

1 Fungi – including moulds and yeasts (see below).

2 Algae – including the green, slimy stuff that you find in ponds.

3 Lichens – actually a partnership between fungi and algae. Often found in tough places like Antarctica – fancy going there for a summer holiday?

MONSTROUS DETAILS: Algae thrive in water filled with sewage. And this is one of their nicer habits...

WANT TO CREATE YOUR OWN ALGAE FARM? DON'T FLUSH THE LOO FOR SIX MONTHS!

Cute little algae?

Some scientists think that algae have their charms, especially the microscopic algae that look like living balls of slime under a microscope. We decided to take them at their word and open up the world's first pet shop for algae...

A QUICK NOTE...

Yes, I know the word "pet" normally means a cute, furry animal but when you've got "plants" that swim around under their own steam, the distinction gets a little blurred.

59

ALGAE-PALS PET SHOP

SLITHER! SPLIT! SLITHER! SPLIT!

Are you a lonely scientist? Are you seeking a little friend, someone who will listen to your latest scientific theories without falling asleep? Look no further! To order – Give us a ring and give us your money!

···◦◦❧◦·· WARNING! ··◦❧◦◦···

Algae breed by splitting in half. You might need to get some other micro creatures to eat your pets before they form a vast, slimy mass that poisons their water ... and *you* if you fall in!

1 Cute ceratium (ser-rat-tee-um)

Description: Looks like a homemade Christmas decoration that's gone wrong.

CHEERS!

Size: 0.5 mm (0.02 inches)

Cute features: Dagger-like spikes for protection from other microscopic creatures.

Feeding: Don't worry about feeding them – they use sunlight and carbon dioxide gas in the air to make sugar for food – a process called photosynthesis (as if you didn't know!).

Note: you can use your pet as a thermometer. The warmer the water, the more they stick their spikes out. This can be useful for working out if your bath is the right temperature!

2 Delightful diatoms
Description: Indescribable – pretty aren't they?

Size: 0.2 mm (0.08 inches)
Delightful features: They shine in the light because they have see-through bodies and hard boxlike outer bodies that contain silica, which also makes up sand and glass.
Feeding: Photosynthesis.

To stop your pets multiplying too much, why not use an animal that looks like a plant? It's wild and wacky...

3 Hungry hydra
Description: A green rubber glove.

Size: 1.25 cm (0.5 inches)
Cute features: Stinging threads in its fingers kill anything that comes near. Er, that's not too cute, is it?
Feeding: "Fingers" grab the prey and bring it into the creature's mouth.

Foul fungal feeding

So you're anti-algae? Oh well, perhaps you'll be fungi-friendly? Enlarged over 500 times through a microscope, fungi look like trendy worms with Afro haircuts. But their eating habits are less pretty – as you're about to find out...

THE FUNGI GUIDE TO ETIQUETTE

by Madame Mould

IF YOU DESIRE TO BE ACCEPTED IN THE BEST HOUSES THEN ETIQUETTE IS ESSENTIAL – SO MIND YOUR MANNERS, MOULDS!

TABLE MANNERS
Eating is very important for fungi – so make sure you eat as much as you can whenever you can. (It's acceptable to burp gas afterwards.)

MUNCH! NIBBLE! SCOFF! CHEW!

BURP! BURP!

Four things not to do
NEVER...
- Ask permission before eating.
- Say "please" or "thank you".
- Ask for a second helping – just help yourself anyway.
- Leave the table (before you've eaten it).

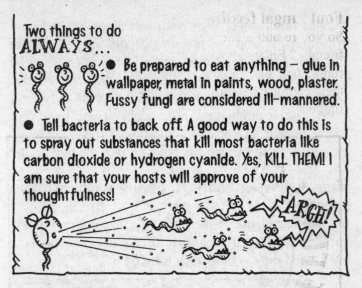

Two things to do
ALWAYS...

● Be prepared to eat anything – glue in wallpaper, metal in paints, wood, plaster. Fussy fungi are considered ill-mannered.

● Tell bacteria to back off. A good way to do this is to spray out substances that kill most bacteria like carbon dioxide or hydrogen cyanide. Yes, KILL THEM! I am sure that your hosts will approve of your thoughtfulness!

ARGH!

Foul fungus facts

1 Dry rot fungus will eat all the wooden bits in your house. It starts by growing in damp areas and extends its feeding tubes into dry areas of walls and floors! The only way to stop it is to cut out huge chunks of your home.

2 A fungus will push anything aside. Its feeding tubes are armoured with chitin, the tough stuff that protects insect bodies and makes beetles so hard to squash.

A TOUGH MATERIAL STOPS US GETTING SQUASHED... IT'S CHITIN!

WHAT D'YOU MEAN, CHEATING? IT'S NOT A FLAMIN' GAME!!

3 Fungi only make small amounts of poisons and they don't harm humans – usually. But before the 1920s the deadly poison arsenic was often added to paints. Fungi ate the paints and sprayed out arsenic gas that smelt of garlic, and some people died.

Sounds fascinating? Well, your rotten spoilsport family will probably stop you breeding deadly fungi or dry rot in your bedroom. Never mind, why not use your microscope to study bugs instead? The rest of this chapter is about really tiny bugs that you can only get a good look at through the microscope. These bugs ain't going to win any beauty contests and their habits are equally repulsive ... are *you* ready to face the ugly truth?

Bugs behaving badly 1: Taking a ride without paying

1 Many bugs have smaller bugs less than 0.2 mm (0.008 inches) long that live on them. Bee mites hang on to ... well, what do you think they hang on to...?

I LIKE IT HERE

YEAH, IT'S THE BEE'S KNEES!

They don't do any harm, so I guess they just think it's a nice place to bee and it gives them a buzz.

2 Feather mites live on birds. There's a type of Mexican parrot that has 30 varieties of feather mite. The bites eat bits of worn feather and dead skin, and if they over eat they probably feel sick as a parrot.

3 A pseudoscorpion hitches lifts on a fly's hairs. If it gets bored of the high life, it brings the fly down to earth with a nasty nip of its poison claws and eats its body!

So you're not afraid to see a pseudoscorpion up close? Well, here's something for you to get your claws into... Who said science wasn't down to earth?

The magic microscope: soil creatures

Soil is alive with bugs and here are two of the most common.

You know what to do ... look very hard...

○

If you can't make out anything yet take a look below. Wow, this microscope is magical! You can really see these bugs...

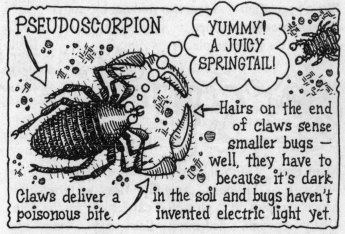

PSEUDOSCORPION

YUMMY! A JUICY SPRINGTAIL!

Hairs on the end of claws sense smaller bugs — well, they have to because it's dark in the soil and bugs haven't invented electric light yet.

Claws deliver a poisonous bite.

The pseudoscorpions eat springtails. (Yes, they really do have springs in their tails and if they were bigger they'd win the world pogo-jumping contest!)

SPRINGTAIL

ARGH! AN EVIL PSEUDOSCORPION!

Spring under abdomen.

Six stubby legs.

Mouth designed for chewing.

So what do you think of the chapter so far? Are you appalled and shocked by the ugliness and the brutality of the bugs featured? You will be. Now here's a never-to-be-repeated opportunity to get the microscopic details on brutal blood-sucking bugs.

Bugs behaving badly 2: Sucking blood

Forget vampires – some bugs make Count Dracula look like a vegetarian – as you can find out by studying them through the microscope.

1 Take fleas for example...

Many types of animal have their own special type of flea – dog fleas on dogs, armadillo fleas on armadillos, hedgehog fleas on ... oh well, I expect you get the point. Oddly enough, hedgehog fleas have their own passengers. Tiny mites hide under their scales. I expect they enjoy life at the sharp end.

2 Flea babies are too small to suck blood but they don't lose out. They eat their parents' poo, which is rich in digested blood. It makes suppertime less of a chore for the parents, but would you really want to eat your dad's poop?

3 One type of flea is called a jigger. It lays its eggs between a person's toes. As it digs a pit in the skin in which to lays its eggs, the female sucks the victim's blood and can introduce germs which cause blood poisoning. I expect the victim says, "Well, I be jiggered!"

A lousy experiment

Our long dead pal Robert Hooke did another revolting experiment with another blood-sucking bug – a louse. Through his microscope he watched a louse sucking blood from his hand into its see-through body. He said:

SUCK!

I could plainly see a small current of blood which came from its snout and poured directly into its belly.

67

I expect the louse was wondering why this funny man was staring at him over lunch.

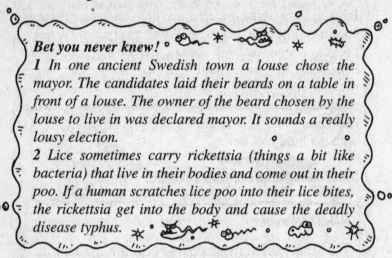

Bet you never knew!
1 In one ancient Swedish town a louse chose the mayor. The candidates laid their beards on a table in front of a louse. The owner of the beard chosen by the louse to live in was declared mayor. It sounds a really lousy election.
2 Lice sometimes carry rickettsia (things a bit like bacteria) that live in their bodies and come out in their poo. If a human scratches lice poo into their lice bites, the rickettsia get into the body and cause the deadly disease typhus.

And by some revolting coincidence we're going to be meeting some murderous microbes in the next chapter. Did I say "coincidence"? Oh well, it's a small world...

MURDEROUS MICROBES

Imagine everything became invisible and the microbes currently invisible began to glow. Everything – trees, houses, people, school dinner and dogs' poo would disappear. But you could still see where they were because the outlines of these objects and almost everything else would be picked out in ghostly glowing microbes. Yes, I'm afraid everything is CRAWLING with the little monsters!

Microscopic monsters fact file

NAME: Microbes

THE BASIC FACTS: The main microbes are... Bacteria, Protozoa, Viruses.

1 Bacteria – see next page.

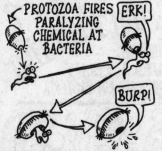

PROTOZOA FIRES PARALYZING CHEMICAL AT BACTERIA

ERK!

BURP!

2 Protozoa change their body shape as they move and engulf bacteria. So if you're tiny don't ask one to come "around" for lunch.

3 Viruses are even smaller so you'll need an electron microscope to spot one. They're basically bundles of DNA (and if you DNA know what I'm talking about turn back to page 44 to refresh your memory).

FLU VIRUS
Attacks cells in the throat (can be a pain in the neck).

MONSTROUS DETAILS: All three can cause deadly diseases.

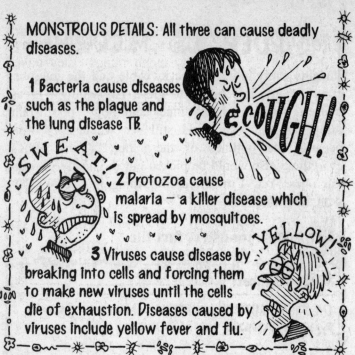

1 Bacteria cause diseases such as the plague and the lung disease TB.

COUGH!

SWEAT!

2 Protozoa cause malaria – a killer disease which is spread by mosquitoes.

3 Viruses cause disease by breaking into cells and forcing them to make new viruses until the cells die of exhaustion. Diseases caused by viruses include yellow fever and flu.

YELLOW!

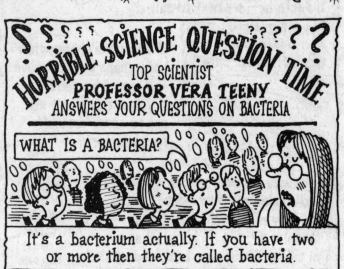

HORRIBLE SCIENCE QUESTION TIME

TOP SCIENTIST
PROFESSOR VERA TEENY
ANSWERS YOUR QUESTIONS ON BACTERIA

WHAT IS A BACTERIA?

It's a bacterium actually. If you have two or more then they're called bacteria.

HUH – DON'T GET SNOTTY WITH US! OK THEN, WHAT **ARE** BACTERIA?

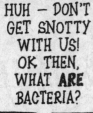

Any one of thousands of types of tiny living things. They have roughly the same features.

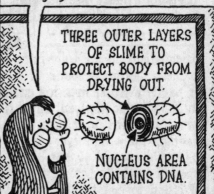

THREE OUTER LAYERS OF SLIME TO PROTECT BODY FROM DRYING OUT.

NUCLEUS AREA CONTAINS DNA.

To get around, bacteria wriggle through the water in which they like to live. Some beat a whip-like tail called a flagellum (fla-gell-lum) and others have tiny beating hairs called cilia (silly-a).

WRIGGLE!

BEAT!

Bacteria come in all shapes and sizes - though, to be honest, they're all pretty tiny. They can be round, and thin, and lemon-shaped, and pear-shaped, and corkscrew-shaped, and square, and comma-shaped and ... oh well ... you get the picture. And you can fit millions in a match box. If you were this small the kitchen table would appear to be 640 km (400 miles) long and getting to school would take for ever!

SO HOW MANY TYPES OF BACTERIA ARE THERE?

Lots

CAN YOU BE MORE EXACT?

No

Scientists from the University of Southern California found 61 types of bacteria living in a hot spring in Yellowstone National Park. 57 were unknown to science. Some scientists think that every pinch of soil could contain 10,000 different types of bacteria but they haven't got round to counting them all yet.

Any volunteers to count them?

Although, we're talking awfully big numbers. An average-sized lawn holds countless billions of individual bacteria — about 4.5 kg (10 lbs) by weight. And they're eaten by an army of tiny creatures such as protozoa and slimy nematode worms with no eyes and six rubbery lips

WHERE ELSE DO BACTERIA LIVE?

Where don't they live! Most bacteria live in "cities" of slime in massive piles like tower blocks 200 micrometres high (that's BIG by their standards). Favourite places for slime cities are — are you ready for this? — sewage pipes, false teeth, contact lenses, the guts and just about anywhere else you can imagine...

SO WHAT DO BACTERIA DO ALL DAY?

Well, they eat and divide to make new bacteria and they eat and divide and when they're bored of that they divide and eat. Well, I suppose they could play football under the microscope but then they might be caught off-slide! Ha, ha — sorry, just my little joke.

MUNCH! SPLIT!

MUNCH! MUNCH!

SPLIT! SPLIT!

A NOTE TO THE READER...

Some people are scared of bacteria. After reading this book you might feel scared too. DON'T. Most do us no harm and some are actually good for us: the bacteria that live in your gut help to make Vitamin K, a substance that helps your blood to clot. Bacteria have been around for thousands of millions of years and they'll still be there at the end of the world. And anyway, they're scientifically fascinating!

Bacteria might be tiny – but they're TOUGH. Their secret is to form spores. These are thick capsules that protect their bodies and they can live for years. You might be surprised to learn that bacteria have really boastful personalities and love bragging about their survival feats. OK, I just made that bit up but just imagine they *were* like this...

Boastful bacteria

Of course, we had it tough when I were a lad. I was stuck for 300 years in a grain of soil stuck to a dried plant...

YAWN!

That's nothing. I remember when I was living on the bottom of a ship and all I had to eat was ... the ship.

MUNCH!

I'd have killed for a bit of ship to eat. I spent years living in a car park and all I had to eat was tarmac.

CHEW!

Well, of course when I was younger I spent 3,000 years living at the bottom of the sea in the freezing cold with enough water pressing down from above to crush a human flat.

SHIVER!

SCOFF!

Huh — you had it soft lad! Before I was in the soil I had to live in central heating pipes and eat them!

74

ALL these boasts are TRUE!

1 Scientists have revived bacteria on plant specimens this old.

2 Bacteria that live in polluted sea water can eat ships! What happens is bacteria in the water eat the sulphur and turn it into sulphide. This joins to iron atoms on the ship to make a black smelly chemical called iron sulphide. Other bacteria happily guzzle this foul mixture – and eat the ship.

3 It's true – some bacteria eat tarmac. Mind you, it takes them hundreds of years to do it – it's a bit like you trying to eat a pile of hamburgers the size of Mount Everest!

4 Bacteria live at the bottom of the sea. But they're so used to the pressure of the water that when they are brought up to the surface where there's less water crushing down on them, their little bodies go pop.

5 Some bacteria like it hot and they're quite happy in your hot copper pipes. They eat the chemical sulphur in the water and poo out a chemical called sulphide which joins with copper atoms in the pipes to make a chemical called copper sulphide that makes the water in your hot taps smell of rotten eggs.

6 Disinfectant contains a chemical called phenol that kills most bacteria – but some bacteria think it's a treat and happily guzzle it!

> ### Bet you never knew!
>
> **1** When bacteria feed inside a dead body, the methane gas they give off makes the body swell up to three times its size. There have even been cases of dead bodies blowing up. A state funeral in 1927 of British King George V's brother-in-law was interrupted by an embarrassing bang as the corpse exploded.
>
> **2** Methane is also made inside cows by bacteria that live in the cow's stomach and digest the tough cell walls of grass. The cow can then digest the grass more easily. Cows get rid of the methane in huge burps or farts. The cows don't mean to be rude but there's no udder choice.

Microscopic expressions

A scientist says:

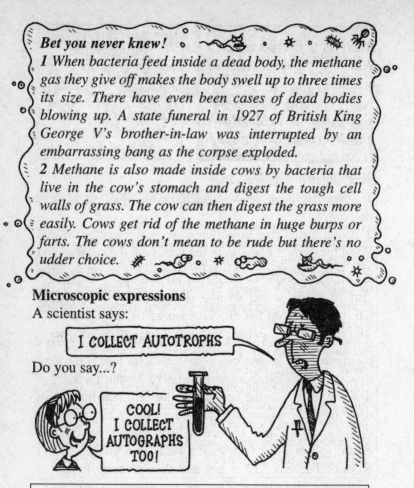

I COLLECT AUTOTROPHS

Do you say...?

COOL! I COLLECT AUTOGRAPHS TOO!

Answer: No. He said *autotrophs* – and if you don't know what they are, keep reading! It's a posh term for being able to make food from simple chemicals – and no, we're not talking cookery lessons here. Autotrophs include plants and certain bacteria that make their food using photosynthesis. (Remember that word? It's on page 60) Other autotrophic bacteria feed off chemicals such as sulphur, as you've just found out...

Bacteria breakfast quiz

Which of these "foods" would bacteria NOT fancy for breakfast...?

a) Your mum's bottle of vitamin C pills.
b) A bucket of sulphuric acid.
c) An old pair of Wellie boots.
d) An ancient temple.

Answers: a) For some reason bacteria don't eat vitamin C. Maybe they don't like healthy foods? **b)** Some bacteria live happily in weak sulphuric acid and can even eat it! **c)** Bacteria happily scoff latex – a kind of tree gum that is the raw material of rubber. During the Second World War many homes burnt down in air raids because bacteria had eaten holes in the fire hoses. The rubber in Wellie boots is treated with sulphur but as you know, some bacteria can eat this chemical. **d)** Angkor in Cambodia is one of the wonders of the world. It's also a giant bacteria snack bar. Bacteria in the soil are making sulphide which is drawn up with moisture into the stones of the temple. More bacteria eat the chemical and poo out an acid that eats away the temple.

Could you be a scientist?

The landlord of a bar in the Yukon, Canada offered his guests a disgusting cocktail. It was champagne ... with a human toe in it complete with toenail. (The toe had been found in a log cabin – no one knew what it was doing there but I expect it was trying to find its feet.) Anyway, the landlord challenged his customers to drink the concoction saying:

But why didn't bacteria eat the toe and make it rot?

a) It was too revolting even for bacteria.

b) It was so cold in the Yukon that the bacteria froze.

c) The toe had been pickled in alcohol and few bacteria can live in these conditions.

Teacher's tea-break teaser

Arm yourself with this treacherously tricky teaser and a pencil and terrorize your teacher's tea-break. Beat out a little tune on the staffroom door. When it opens smile an angelic smile and ask:

The magic microscope

An old pair of leather shoes.
Not much to look at perhaps
but they hide a fascinating
range of tiny life forms.
Looks like another case for
the magic microscope...

Take a look. Oh, go on! The shoes don't smell too bad!
Now take a look below... And here you see the secrets
that lurk on a humble pair of shoes. The leather looks like
crazy paving and...

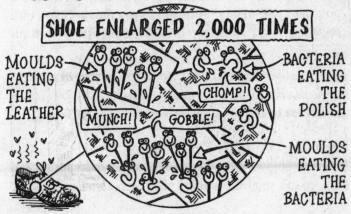

SHOE ENLARGED 2,000 TIMES

MOULDS
EATING
THE
LEATHER

CHOMP!

MUNCH! GOBBLE!

BACTERIA
EATING
THE
POLISH

MOULDS
EATING
THE
BACTERIA

Dare you discover ... how to provide a snug, cosy home for bacteria?

What you need:

A screw-topped jar filled with water.
Some grass.

What you do:

1 Allow the water to stand for three hours.
2 Cut the grass into little pieces and add it to the water. Replace the top.
3 Leave the jar in a warm place for a week.

What do you notice?

a) The liquid has gone cloudy.
b) The liquid has gone green.
c) The liquid has gone frothy and orange and is escaping from the jar and eating everything in sight.

Answer: a) The cloudiness is made by millions of bacteria happily eating the grass. The bacteria were on the grass and in the air before you sealed the jar. Empty the jar outside and round up a grown-up to wash it with disinfectant. If **c)** then CONGRATULATIONS, you've discovered a new form of bacteria... Now get out fast!

Anyway, we're going to tear ourselves away from the slimy world of bacteria now. Don't worry, they'll plop up pretty nastily in the next chapter. But right now we're moving on to the equally slimy world of protozoa.

Prowling protozoa

The first person to spot protozoa under the microscope (they're too small to see any other way) was our old pal

Leeuwenhoek. Wanna know what he saw? Here's what a protozoan looks like (one is a protozoan – two are protozoa)...

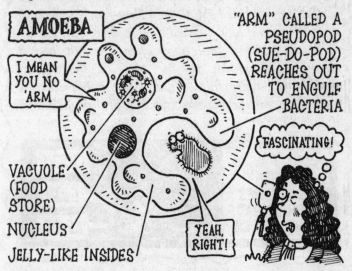

Dare you discover ... how to make an amoeba?
What you need:
A paper hankie (not a snotty one).
That's it.

What you do:
1 Make two tears 4 cm (1.5 inches) long in each side of the hankie. (This will help to make an amoeba-like shape in the water.)
2 Screw the hankie up tightly.
3 Twist any sticking out points of hankie into points to make an amoeba shape.
4 Put it in water. If you stir the water around your amoeba will appear to move. BEWARE, it might engulf your finger! And if you find that hard to swallow read this...

Bet you never knew!

Protozoa can breed very fast. For example, paramecium (pa-ra-me-see-um) divides every 22 hours. If one started splitting on New Year's Day, by 7 March it would have formed a huge slimy ball 1.6 km (one mile) across. Little more than a month later it would have grown to the size of the Earth! Fortunately, other tiny creatures are public-spirited enough to eat the paramecium before they take over the world!

WELL, I WISH THE TINY CREATURES WOULD EAT A BIT FASTER!

OOER!

ERK!

ARGH!

AN URGENT NOTE TO THE READER...

Do you walk on the grass? Well, don't. IF YOU WALK ON THE GRASS MILLIONS OF INNOCENT TINY CREATURES WILL DIE!!!! Your feet squash the soil and push moisture out of it and this causes the slime moulds to appear!

"So what's a slime mould?" I hear you ask nervously. Well, don't feel too anxious – slime moulds are harmless to humans and you probably didn't eat one in your school dinner the other day. But if you're still curious, this slime mould's autobiography should answer all your questions...

82

MY LIFE AS A SLIME MOULD

By A Meeba
Published by Slimy & Creep

I don't remember when I was born because I was very young at the time. But I was certainly an amoeba - I only became part of a slime mould later on. I loved playing in the dark, murky soil - well, it's where my roots are! And although I didn't have too many friends there were always bacteria to keep me company - until I gobbled them up!

One day a kid walked over the lawn. I felt a huge rumble and a crash and a shaking and the soil became so dry that the bacteria stopped dividing. Soon my vacuole was rumbling. Then I saw another amoeba. This amoeba made a chemical signal and I felt drawn to follow it. And soon there was another amoeba following me and before I knew it I was part of a long line of amoebas. "Oh goodie!" I thought. "Let's go line dancing!"

Soon we were flowing together (still under the ground, of course). So I just went with the flow until we oozed into a slug shape. "Wow!" I thought. "I've always wanted to be a gastropod!"

Editor's note: This formation is actually called a "slug" and it's a form of slime-mould.

Editor's note: That's the posh name for a slug.

We crept onwards. Behind us was a glistening trail of

slime made out of the jelly-like insides of amoebas that had been trampled in the rush and ripped to bits on sharp grains of earth. What an heroic sacrifice - those amoebas really had guts! Well, I could see them!

On the way I chatted to the other amoebas and they said the world was ending. So I asked the others where we were heading but no one knew. Then one old amoeba mumbled something about heading to the light and heat - or did she say we were going for a light eat? I'd have happily murdered a few bacteria for breakfast! When we got to the surface I was gob-smacked - I'd never seen anything like it in my entire life (Oh, all right, I hadn't seen much at all in my life!) It was a slimy tower made of living, squishing, squirming amoebas! It was vast, it was huge, IT WAS GIGANTIC! It must have been - hmm, let me think - all of one-tenth of a millimetre high!

Thousands of millions of amoebas were piling together higher and higher. Groaning noises came from deep inside the pile and wild rumours flew amongst us that millions of amoebas were making a hard chemical that turned their bodies stiff and killing themselves just to make sure our lovely tower didn't topple over!

I started climbing. Higher and higher I crawled, past the groaning amoebas who were turning themselves into hard lumps, past the amoebas who were holding up countless others. Call me ambitious but I just had to get to the top! As I climbed I noticed that I too was changing. My body was becoming hard and tough. "OOPS!" I thought, "It's tough at the top." But no, I was growing a capsule. A space capsule to protect my body. Then I was on top of the tower and I felt the wind. A breath of air blew me away and all I remember was a buffeting on my capsule - but I'd escaped the end of the world! I was shaking like a bag of jelly! (Well, maybe that's because I am a bag of jelly?)

Eventually I landed in this nice damp bit of earth with plenty of bacteria. But I was lucky - 99.9 per cent of the amoebas didn't make it. I might be a humble amoeba but I'm a survivor and that makes me a bit special, in my own small way...

THE END

SCIENTIFIC NOTE...
And all this happens because YOU walked on the grass! Scientists aren't too sure of the details but amoebas form slime moulds in dry conditions. The process is controlled by chemicals that amoebas make themselves.

Had enough of microbes yet? Well, tough – they haven't had enough of you! At this very second there are several million crawling over your face and exploring your nostrils. And if you wanna know what else they're up to you'd better read on!

Because from now it's gonna get personal...

MEDICAL MICROSCOPES

Where would modern medical science be without the microscope? Up a blind alley, that's where! Without microscopes scientists couldn't spot the more interesting little details of the body that really make it tick – like flakes of skin, for example. Chances are you've already seen a few of these disgusting details...

Imagine a summer's morning. A speck of dust dances in the sunlight like a gilded gnat. It's a perfect moment ... *until you realize what dust is actually made of...*

Dare you discover ... what dust is made of?
What you need:
A shaft of sunlight. (Draw some dark curtains allowing only a gap of 15 cm (6 inches). Alternatively, wait until night and use a small bright torch.

What you do:
1 Face the light.
2 Brush your hands through your hair, brush your hands over your arms, then lift your shirt and give it a shake.

What do you notice?
a) A cloud of black dots comes off me.
b) A cloud of shiny dots comes off me.
c) Huge chunks of skin fall off my body.

Bet you never knew!
Specks of dust are some of the smallest things you can see. They're just 20 micrometres across and not much larger than bacteria. They're floating around all the time but you can't see them unless the light glints on them.

So, how well do you know your body? Just take a really close look at your hair, your eyes, your skin colour, the shape of your nose, the location of any moles or freckles. Spotted anything new? Well, in actual fact there's a lot you've never seen ... the tiny bits.

Could you be a scientist?
Scientists estimate that you lose 50,000 bits of skin every *minute*. But the most incredible thing is that they've found that skin flakes from a man have about five times as many germs as skin flakes from a woman. Why? Is it because...

a) Male sweat has more food in it so more germs can live on male skin?
b) Men are dirtier than women?
c) Germs are killed by perfume on a woman's skin?

87

Would you like to explore the human body in grisly detail? Well, if you're a bacterium you'd be doing this all the time and loving it! For bacteria, every day's a holiday...

THE INCREDIBLE BODY TOUR...

HORRIBLE SCIENCE and
Bacteria Breakaways present...

The get away from it all (but not very far) tour
It's the ultimate mini-break on

THE HUMAN SKIN & HAIR!

"I had a rotten time and enjoyed every minute of it" A. Bacterium.

ITINERARY

DAY ONE

Morning: First stop is the mouth for a quick tour of the tongue. Marvel at the sight of 9,000 tastebuds in clusters, some with round tops like mushrooms

and others pointed and ideal for moving food around. Enjoy the sight of the playful local bacteria frolicking amongst the tastebuds!

Afternoon: Sign up for the fascinating microbe safari. Watch the different bacteria in between the teeth. But beware – amoebas lurk in this area and they might try to eat you!

NOTES

1 Chinese leader Mao Tse-tung (1893-1976) never brushed his teeth and they eventually turned green. Eek by gum, I bet Mao just had to green and bear it.

2 The amoebas eat bacteria and are harmless to humans. One place to get a free amoeba is a dog's mouth. When a friendly dog gives you a big slobbery kiss you get an amoeba thrown in too.

DAY TWO

Morning: Enjoy a relaxing walking tour of the skin! Carefully does it – in some teenagers the skin pumps out half a bucket of oil a day so the going might get a bit slippery! Feel free to snack on the delicious oil and any dead bits of skin you might find.

Afternoon: Admire the volcanoes on the face plain. Well, they're not really volcanoes, they're pimples – so watch out when they erupt pus!

Evening: Slake your thirst at the sweat gland cocktail bar. The local tipple (sweat) is a great tonic for us bacteria. It's full of delicious salts and sugars and minerals to keep us healthy!

> **~NOTE~**
>
> With more than two million sweat bars you're spoilt for choice but beware - women make nice easy-to-drink little sweat droplets, but men can make giant globules that splash onto the floor!

DAY THREE

Morning: Explore the enchanting hair forest. There's always something new to see – like exciting split ends that look like splintered wood or the cute new hairs that look like pink worms emerging from the soil. Let's hope it's not a bad hair day!

SPOOKY!

GUZZLE!

Lunch: Dine on delicious fresh dandruff washed down with fatty oil from the hair.

Afternoon: Admire the fine collection of dust and pollen sticking to the oil on the hair tree trunks. (It's the oil that gives unwashed hair that lovely greasy shine.) If we're particularly lucky we might see some nits (louse eggs) or that shy retiring creature, the human head louse, with its hairy body, jointed legs and feelers and crab-like shell. Unforgettable!

LOOK, OVER THERE!

Evening: That's the end of the tour. Time to hop off the skin and take an air tour of the house before landing on the cat.

More tours

1 THE EYEBALL CELLS EXPERIENCE

Feast your eyes on the cornea with its patchwork of cells like a tiled roof. Seeing is believing as you'll see with the see-through cells of the lens arranged in lines like a venetian blind. (If they weren't see-through the human would be blind instead!)

2 THE BONE BREAKAWAY

Tour the eerie world inside the bones. The spongy bone inside the hard outer layer is like an immense cave system full of inter-connecting tunnels. You'd be a bone-head to miss it!

3 THE LONG LUNG WEEKEND

Visit the lungs for a breath of fresh air! Explore the tiny tubes into which air flows and admire the alveoli. These are the bags 0.01 cm (0.004 inches) across surrounded with blood vessels where oxygen goes into the blood and carbon dioxide flows out! Bags of fun for all the family!

WARNING: The walls of the tubes are lined with snot and you risk being stuck and then coughed up!

But if you didn't fancy taking a bacterial break then there's another way to see the human body. You could shrink down to the size of MI Gutzache. Let's check out where he's got to... Can you remember where we left him?

It's a small world! (continued)

The story so far. A shrinking experiment has gone horribly wrong and intrepid private eye Gutzache is floating in a cloud of snot...

Gutzache could see where he was going and he didn't relish it one bit. Tiny movements in the air puffed him towards the massive furry form of the Professor's cat, Tiddles. Gutzache drifted through a forest of tree trunks – at least, that's how it appeared to him. In fact, it was the fur on the cat's back.

Cats. Don't ask why but they're not my favourite animals. If things had worked out different I'd have taken my chances with organized crime. But I was on the cat and at least it was warm. Then she started licking herself. I felt rough but her tongue looked rougher – in fact, it was more like a giant rubbery sheet covered in cat dribble with spikes as long as my fingers.

So Gutzache was on Tiddles? How clever of her to rescue him! The cat's rough tongue acts like a comb separating the hairs and making glands in her skin produce oils that keep the fur in good condition. The spit dries (or evaporates as we scientists say) off the hairs, taking away heat and cooling her down.

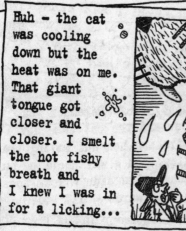

Huh – the cat was cooling down but the heat was on me. That giant tongue got closer and closer. I smelt the hot fishy breath and I knew I was in for a licking...

LICK!

But just when all seemed lost Gutzache was rescued by a rather unlikely helper. Well, it wasn't so much of a helper as something that just came along and Gutzache grabbed hold of it and held on tight. It had a huge shield-shaped body about three times larger than Gutzache, covered in armoured plates. It had a dagger-like feeding tube and inside its see-through body Gutzache glimpsed a mass of freshly swallowed blood. Suddenly, the creature sprang high into the air – to Gutzache it seemed higher than a skyscraper. He had hitched a ride on a flea!

My whole life flashed before my eyes – it didn't make for pretty viewing. Then my stomach lurched as the flea touched down on another part of the cat's back. "Life's full of ups and downs," I thought, hastily jumping free and fleeing the flea.

I had no idea where Gutzache was and I was looking everywhere! I had divided the room into squares and I was searching each one using the strongest magnifying glass I could find. Where had he got to?

Nearer than you thought, Prof. Remember you were down on the floor and the cat came up? Maybe you remember stroking her and saying the words: "Naughty Tiddles, don't walk here – you might tread on Gutzache!" You didn't look too hard at your fingers afterwards – did you?

ER, NO!

Well, I was on one of them! You picked me up from the cat's back. You stood up – I was hollering like crazy, something like, "Listen up you stupid scientist I'm on your finger!" But you didn't hear me!

The Professor's skin was full of cracks like dried mud. Here and there tiny pits bubbled oily beads of moisture. Meanwhile Gutzache was sweating too.

It was an ugly situation and the Prof wasn't too pretty neither. The hand was going up. I clung to a hair on the back of a finger. I knew it was going to be bad - I just didn't know how bad. But then I saw where we were headed and I knew. The giant mouth opened and a blast of hot air hit me. My stomach heaved — it smelt of sour milk, strong cheese, onions, garlic and old cow pats. Round globs of spit and slimy bacteria flew towards me. The Prof could sure use some mouthwash.

YUK!

Honestly, this is too bad, I DO NOT HAVE BAD BREATH! It is nonetheless a fascinating fact that every human breath contains hundreds of bacteria from the mouth. Of course, I still had no idea that Gutzache was on my finger...

ERK!

The Prof's nails didn't look in too good a shape. They were rough as tree bark and the ends were jagged. Bite marks I thought. I was right.

Helpless with horror, Gutzache watched as the Professor's finger was inserted into his giant mouth. The teeth looked like huge yellow cliffs and here and there slimy bacteria nestled in their folds and ridges. The teeth began to work backwards and forwards and the nail buckled and bent under the chewing action.

The job had become a gross-out. At that moment I longed to be anywhere but where I was. Well, maybe not anywhere – I'd give the Prof's guts a miss. Meantime, the Prof was making a meal of them fingernails. °∘∘...

Actually, nails are made of keratin. Seen through an electron microscope keratin looks like a rope with smaller chemicals wound around it. This makes it very hard to tear and that's why my nail was buckling and not breaking.

Meanwhile Gutzache was right under the Professor's nose – literally. The finger didn't seem too safe so he decided to climb up a thick rope. It turned out to be one of the Professor's nostril hairs and it was encrusted with dried snot. Feeling faint Gutzache swung himself into the hot, windy nostril and then clambered higher up the cheek.

The Prof and me were face to face but he still couldn't see me. He had some cheek! But the worst of all, his skin was crawling. It was oozing with slimy balls of bacteria that hid in tiny cracks. I figured I'd crack too if I stuck around. So I thought about it plenty but I couldn't figure how to escape...

I had no idea all this time that Gutzache was on my face. Interestingly, over two million bacteria live on the cheeks and nose - and 72 million live in the grease on the forehead. Well, not that I've counted them ... but perhaps Gutzache could be persuaded to make a small survey...

Hey, I'd rather bungee jump off Brooklyn Bridge! The Prof still hadn't spotted me but something else had. It had a body like an armoured car and eight legs and a face that would sink a battleship. It wasn't too fast but for a minute I thought I was chicken-feed. But the bug wasn't too bothered - it was eating the squirming things off the Prof's skin. I said, "You're welcome pal!"

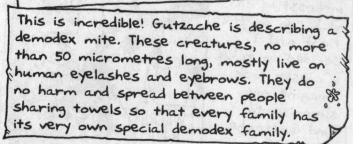

This is incredible! Gutzache is describing a demodex mite. These creatures, no more than 50 micrometres long, mostly live on human eyelashes and eyebrows. They do no harm and spread between people sharing towels so that every family has its very own special demodex family.

But things were about to get even worse for Gutzache. The Professor frowned as he wondered what to do next. He decided to resume his search of the floor, but the damage had been done. His skin rumpled and crinkled as if moved by an earthquake and tiny chunks dislodged themselves and slipped into the air – a perfectly normal event caused by frowning. Once more, Gutzache felt himself falling helplessly – this time gripping on for dear life to what looked like a giant cornflake but was actually a flake of skin...

Gutzache landed on the very microscope slide that he had been sneezed off at the start of his adventure. And a minute or two later a familiar face peered down at him through the microscope...

The Prof enlarged me. He was talking about me taking a dip in a drop of pond water. Two seconds later I gave him my considered reply – "I don't swim," I snapped. And with that I quit. After what happened today it was small wonder ... a very, very small wonder.

FORGET IT!

If YOU don't fancy shrinking as small as Gutzache in order to check out some body bits, you could always look at them through a microscope. Surgeons use microscopes all the time for what's called microsurgery. This can involve re-attaching bits and pieces of the body that have been chopped off by accident. Hey – d'you fancy a bash at microsurgery? This quiz will have you in stitches!

Could you be a microsurgeon?

Unfortunately, your teacher has cut off his little finger. It happened whilst he was showing your class how to use a microtome. Even more unfortunately you're the only person who can help – but you've got to answer these questions correctly...

WHO ME?

1 You hastily prepare the operating theatre. Why do you need a video camera and monitor linked up to a microscope?

a) So you can make a souvenir video to show your friends.

b) So you can see what you're doing without having to peer through the microscope all the time.

c) So other doctors can watch your progress and give you advice.

2 OK, you're ready for the op but how are you going to re-attach the finger?

a) Superglue.

b) Sew it back on using a tiny needle.

c) Put it in a special bandage to hold it in place and wait two weeks for the finger to grow back on to the hand.

3 How do you join up the smaller blood vessels?

a) They're too small to bother about.

b) Melt the ends and weld them together.

c) Use a tiny staplegun.

4 After the operation you're keen to keep the blood flowing into your teacher's little finger. If the blood clots or fails to flow then the finger could die and become rotten and drop off. So how do you keep the blood flowing?

a) Suspend your teacher upside down with his finger pointing downwards.

b) Get a huge hungry slimy leech to suck the blood from the little finger so that more rushes in.

c) Rub the finger so that the blood rushes into it.

Answers:

All the answers are **b)**.

1 Sometimes surgeons use special microscopes with several eyepieces so that they can all see what's going on without shoving each other out of the way and taking turns.

2 The trick is to use a tiny needle the size of this dash – with thread 0.2 mm wide to sew together all the nerves and blood vessels and bits of flesh that have been cut. Got all that? Good, well get going then. And no, you can't practise first.

3 Electrical probes are used for this delicate job.

4 It's true – leeches are often used after microsurgery because their spit contains a substance that stops blood clotting and keeps it on the move.

What your score means...

0-1 You're a public menace who should not be allowed within 50 km of an operating theatre. Your poor teacher may need another operation to repair the damage...

2-3 OK, but I'm still a bit worried you might sew your teacher's finger on the wrong hand.

4 Go for it!

HORRIBLE HEALTH WARNING!

You're not going to practise microsurgery on your little brother or sister, are you? Put that scalpel down at once!

Even whilst the surgeons are battling to save your teacher's finger another group of scientists are glued to their microscopes as they take a closer look at the human body. Who are they and what are they up to? Well, I'd like to tell you now but I can't because ... the answer's in the next chapter!

PSST, IT'S A SECRET!

SECRET CELLS

The amazing thing about the body is that the closer you look, the more you see. Seen close the body is an amazing landscape of hills and forests – oh all right, they're goosebumps and hairs – but seen closer still, it's an even more incredible assembly of ... cells.

You remember cells? Robert Hooke was discovering them on page 58. Well, now it's time to look at animal and especially human cells. Here's the vital facts you need to get started...

Microscopic monsters fact file

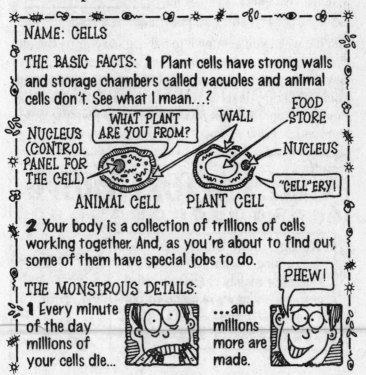

NAME: CELLS

THE BASIC FACTS: **1** Plant cells have strong walls and storage chambers called vacuoles and animal cells don't. See what I mean...?

WHAT PLANT ARE YOU FROM?

NUCLEUS (CONTROL PANEL FOR THE CELL)

WALL

FOOD STORE

NUCLEUS

"CELL"ERY!

ANIMAL CELL   PLANT CELL

2 Your body is a collection of trillions of cells working together. And, as you're about to find out, some of them have special jobs to do.

THE MONSTROUS DETAILS:

1 Every minute of the day millions of your cells die...

PHEW!

...and millions more are made.

2 Your mouth cells only last a few days and then they flake off into your spit and get swallowed and eaten – so you actually eat tiny bits of your own body. Eat too many and you'd be much too full of yourself! Other cells stick around longer. Liver cells, for example, liver longer – up to five years.

WHAT ARE YOU EATING, JENKINS?

MYSELF, MISS!

But it's when you get down to the real nitty-gritty of cells that they become truly amazing. Each cell is like a tiny factory – in fact, it's so like a factory that you could imagine it is a factory. We've asked factory boss and Supreme Chief Executive Dick Taytor to guide us round...

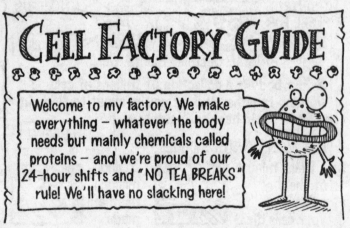

CELL FACTORY GUIDE

Welcome to my factory. We make everything – whatever the body needs but mainly chemicals called proteins – and we're proud of our 24-hour shifts and "NO TEA BREAKS" rule! We'll have no slacking here!

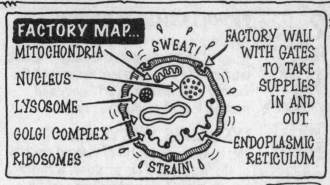

FACTORY MAP...

- MITOCHONDRIA
- NUCLEUS
- LYSOSOME
- GOLGI COMPLEX
- RIBOSOMES

SWEAT!

FACTORY WALL WITH GATES TO TAKE SUPPLIES IN AND OUT.

ENDOPLASMIC RETICULUM

STRAIN!

First stop, my office – known as "THE NUCLEUS". Here are the DNA computers that send the orders to those lazy workers on the shopfloor.

DO THIS!

DO THAT!

MITOCHONDRIA POWER STATIONS

GENERATE!

Here in the cell factory we generate our own power. Don't ask me how we do it – I'm only the boss! It's all done with glucose and oxygen and the end-product is ATP* (That's a little energy brick chemical that can be broken to release power whenever it's needed in the cell.)

KEEP OUT!

GOLGI COMPLEX

That's our storeroom for proteins.

RIBOSOMES

"TOIL!"

This is where the real work is done. The workers put together protein that the cell needs to grow. Nice work guys and no, you can't have a pay rise!

"WORK!"

*SCIENTIFIC NOTE...

ATP is adenosine triphosphate (ad-deeno-sin tri-foss-fate). Say this in a science lesson and the shock could make your teacher's wig fall off!

ENDOPLASMIC RETICULUM

(En-do-plas-mic ret-tick-u-lum) We're proud of this underground railway. It boosts productivity by taking proteins around the factory with maximum efficiency and minimal loss of productive capacity.

LYSOSOME WASTE PLANT

This is where we get rid of clapped out bits of the factory and I'm afraid we sometimes have to get rid of workers here too. But don't worry, they're dissolved in acid and it's quite painless really.

BUSINESS STRATEGY

When the factory gets too big we divide it down the middle into two separate enterprises. It's a big job because we have to copy everything in the factory including the nucleus and DNA computers but it's worth it to double production output.

STAGES OF DIVISION → CELL • CELL IN FIGURE OF 8 • TWO CELLS

Bet you never knew!
If a nucleus from a cell on the end of your nose was the size of your local park, the atoms that make up water will still be smaller than a postage stamp but your head would be the size of planet Earth! Know anyone that big-headed?

So you don't fancy working in the cell factory? Well, if you're looking for something to do, Dick Taytor has recommended some interesting openings for body cells...

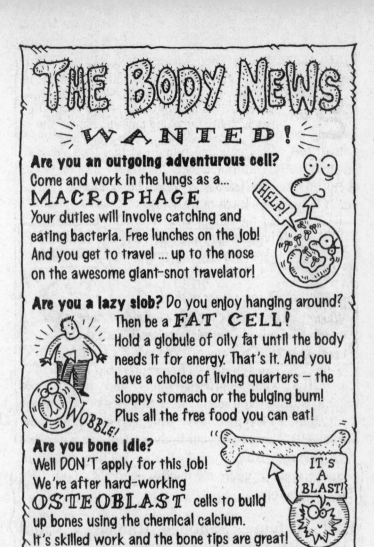

THE BODY NEWS

⚡ WANTED! ⚡

Are you an outgoing adventurous cell?
Come and work in the lungs as a...
MACROPHAGE
Your duties will involve catching and
eating bacteria. Free lunches on the job!
And you get to travel ... up to the nose
on the awesome giant-snot travelator!

HELP!

Are you a lazy slob? Do you enjoy hanging around?
Then be a **FAT CELL!**
Hold a globule of oily fat until the body
needs it for energy. That's it. And you
have a choice of living quarters – the
sloppy stomach or the bulging bum!
Plus all the free food you can eat!

WOBBLE!

Are you bone idle?
Well DON'T apply for this job!
We're after hard-working
OSTEOBLAST cells to build
up bones using the chemical calcium.
It's skilled work and the bone tips are great!

IT'S A BLAST!

Scientific cell-spotters

It took ages for scientists to realize how important cells
were to living things. One of the first to make the
connection was German scientist Theodor Schwann

(1810-1882). Young Theo was a revoltingly good little child who was brilliant at school and kind to everyone he knew. YUCK! When he grew up he became a scientist and discovered that yeasts make alcoholic drinks by feeding on sugars and making alcohol. He also studied lots of bits of animals and found out that they were all made of cells. Unfortunately Schwann's views on yeasts were attacked by jealous rival scientists and he got so upset he gave up much of his work.

Gradually, with improved stains and microscopes scientists discovered many different types of cells in the body. But they lost their nerve with one type of cell ... the nerve cells. Nerves are your body's telephone wires that take messages to and from the brain – but they were hard to make sense of under the microscope.

That was before...

Hall of fame: Santiago Ramon y Cajal (1852-1934) Nationality: Spanish

Young Santiago was a sensitive artistic lad who wanted to be an artist. His dad was less sensitive and less artistic and wanted his son to be a doctor like him. But the boy rebelled and played truant from school. Don't try this – you might not get away with it.

Santiago didn't. He was punished by being sent to work for a shoemaker. (It must have given him a terrible sense of de-feet.) Santiago decided that medicine wasn't so bad after all, and so the boy and his dad studied medicine together. But they had a problem – there was a shortage of skeletons to use to study bones and the family were too poor to buy them.

What did they do?

a) Made shoes and sold them to buy bones.

THESE'LL GET US TWO HIP BONES AND A SET OF RIBS!

b) Killed people and studied their bones.

c) Dug up bones in the local churchyard.

PRAY! PRAY!

HURRY UP, THEY'LL BE COMING OUT IN A MINUTE!

Answer:
c) This was a grave crime and they had to do it at *dead of night* – geddit? If the local priest had found out he'd have had a bone to pick with the pair of them!

After boning up on his medical knowledge Santiago's dad became a professor and after a spell in the army medical service Santiago studied at his dad's university. By the 1880s Santiago was really into microscopes, but he had a problem. Here's what his diary might have looked like...

JANUARY 1888

These nerves are getting on my nerves. I'm trying to study them but they're all tangled up and I can't see where one begins and one ends. Scientists reckon they're long fibres like bits of string but its hard to be sure and I'm getting in a real tangle! I'm a bag of nerves!

FEBRUARY 1888

I've heard about a new discovery by Italian scientist, Camille Golgi.* He was mixing up chemicals in a hospital kitchen and cooked up this stain to show nerves clearly. It's based on silver nitrate. Hmm, I thought, that was the chemical used to develop photos. It could be an exciting development, but all the other scientists think it's useless.

MARCH 1888

mumble!

mutter, moan!

WOW AND WOW AGAIN! It was tough to get the stain to work - it's hard to mix and get the right quantity. But I've done it - and guess what! I can see the nerves clearly! I was really nervous that it wouldn't work but now I can see that the nerves are a network of cells. I can't wait to tell everyone!

APRIL 1888

I don't believe it - I've sent my account of the discovery to a science magazine and they haven't

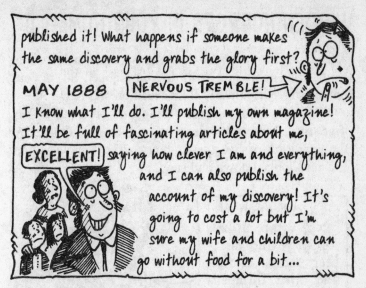

published it! What happens if someone makes the same discovery and grabs the glory first?

MAY 1888 NERVOUS TREMBLE!

I know what I'll do. I'll publish my own magazine! It'll be full of fascinating articles about me, EXCELLENT! saying how clever I am and everything, and I can also publish the account of my discovery! It's going to cost a lot but I'm sure my wife and children can go without food for a bit...

* Yes, he *was* something to do with the Golgi complex – he discovered it!

The magazine was in Spanish, a language most foreign scientists didn't understand, but eventually the news of the discovery got around. Santiago became famous, and in 1906 he and Golgi were awarded the Nobel Prize. But they were still arguing about nerves because Golgi still reckoned they were fibres.

Mind you, looking at dead nerve cells isn't half as scary as peering at the creatures in the next chapter. They're the most disgustingly ugly microscopic monsters of them all! Unfortunately these little monsters share your home and no, I'm NOT talking about your little brother or sister here!

Will your nerve hold for the next chapter?

HIDDEN HORRORS IN YOUR HOME

This is a chapter about the microscopic monsters that haunt your home and skulk in your supper. So, is your home as safe as houses? Better read on and find out!

Well, one thing's certain: things are better than they used to be. Almost 400 years ago a guest was shocked at the condition of his guest's house. The famous writer Erasmus looked down and saw:

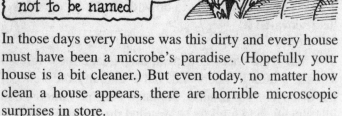

...a collection of spit, vomit, urine of dogs and men, beer, scraps of fish and other filthiness not to be named.

In those days every house was this dirty and every house must have been a microbe's paradise. (Hopefully your house is a bit cleaner.) But even today, no matter how clean a house appears, there are horrible microscopic surprises in store.

Like these.

Five hidden horrors in your home

1 For every 0.03 cubic metres (cubic foot) of air in your home there are 300,000 tiny floating lumps of grit, dead skin, ash and rubber. You breathe this lot in all the time but luckily most of it gets stuck in your wonderful snotty throat.

2 Have you got a cat? If so, when it licks itself tiny globules of spit will be released in invisible clouds. In a few hours of grooming your cat will have produced several billion balls of spit that float gracefully through the air and splatter every surface in the house with kitty drool.

3 If you've got a dog your house may be littered with dog hairs. You'll get more of them in the spring when the dog moults and you might see there are two different types: ordinary hairs and longer hairs that help protect the others and help them trap warm air next to the dog's skin. Oh, nearly forgot – attached to the hairs you'll find clumps of rotting doggie dandruff.

4 And that's not all. If you're really unlucky your dog might have dog lice. There'll be tiny eggs on the hairs and lots of little 1.5 mm-long flea-like creatures keen to explore your home and make new friends.

ALL DOGS ARE LOUSY!

5 Under your carpet you might find "woolly bears". No, these aren't large grizzly teddies that roam the forests of North America – they're grisly little carpet-beetle grubs that happily chomp their way through your carpets. They relish a nice dollop of cat fluff or dog hair or even human hair – well, carpets for breakfast, lunch and supper must get a bit boring. Mind you, if your parents find them they'll be chewing the carpet too.

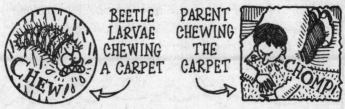

BEETLE LARVAE CHEWING A CARPET

PARENT CHEWING THE CARPET

CHEW!!

CHOMP!

But that's nothing. *Nothing* to what else lurks in your carpets...

The magic microscope

It's time to switch on the magic microscope and take a look at this pinch of dust from a vacuum cleaner bag. Take a look in the circle. Go on, you know you want to...

o

OK, now keep reading – if you dare!

DUST ENLARGED 7,000 TIMES

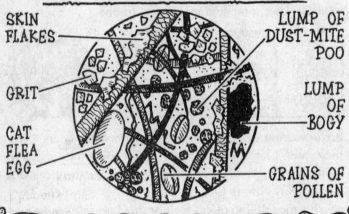

SKIN FLAKES

GRIT

CAT FLEA EGG

LUMP OF DUST-MITE POO

LUMP OF BOGY

GRAINS OF POLLEN

Bet you never knew!
Your home is swarming with tiny creatures – called dust mites. These bugs don't do any harm but we can breathe in their poo and this can trigger asthma attacks in some people that make breathing hard. And the really bad news is that dust mites poo 20 times a day (If they used toilet paper it would cost a fortune!)

Could you be a scientist?

In 1973 physician Dr Robert Haddock found a fishy mystery on the island of Guam. Cases of food poisoning by salmonella bacteria were soaring but why? The islanders were eating the same food as usual – it was mostly brought to the island in tins and free of bacteria. So how were bacteria getting into the food? Eventually the doctor discovered the truth.

But what was it?

a) People weren't washing their hands after visiting the toilet and the germs were on their hands when they cooked the food.

b) Cats were spreading the germs by leaping on to the dinner table and dribbling over the food.

c) Vacuum cleaners were sucking up the germs and spraying them everywhere.

Answer:

c) Yes – I'm sorry to say that when you vacuum the floor tiny things like germs get sucked in the cleaner and because they're very small they get through the bag and the filter and out the exhaust pipe and spray all over you. Actually, it's even *worse* than that because along with the germs emerges a huge cloud of mite poo from the mites in the carpet! Meantime any sucked-up baby mites stay in the cleaner bag and happily dine on the vast collection of scrumptious dead skin they find there!

What are you saying "yuck" for? You've helped with the hoovering haven't you? It didn't kill you – did it? Well, your body can fight off the germs and the mite poo mostly gets stuck in the snot of your nose and throat so it's not an excuse to refuse to help with the cleaning.

Bet you never knew!
Hold on to this book, sit down and take a deep breath. Ready now? I've got a bit of bad news ... you know those revolting mite things in the carpet? Well, they're not just in the carpet. There's some in your bed and in your pillow and there's even worse news to come ... you'd best read on!

MUNCH!

CHOMP!

CRAWL!

POO!

PLOP!

CREEP!

A quick note to the reader...

Remember what I said about bacteria? Don't panic! Mites have been living with humans since the day when people lived in caves and the Internet was just a smart way to catch mammoths. And they've never done us any harm! (That's the mites not the mammoths.)

Let's imagine a dust mite wrote letters to her friend on the carpet. OK, I know this is a mite silly – after all I expect dust mites use mobile phones these days...

To Cara Petmite,
The carpet.

The Pillow.

Dear Cara,
Greetings from Pillowtown! It's comfy here and everything's fine. Trouble is a giant human insists on getting into bed with us every night and he snores! Mind you, the night life's great - there's 40,000 of us and I've got loads of mites. How's things with you?
Your mite,
Pilla Mite

HI!

← SOME OF MY MITES

Dear Cara,
As I was saying it's great - I've got the whole family with me including grandma and great grandma. Great-great-grandma's dead now but I see her mouldering body every time I go for a poo. And there's loads of food!.

CHOMP!

Actually that's all down to the human I mentioned. The human lays on dead skin and grease and tasty dried dribble for us to eat. Is that generous or what? And the human even keeps us warm - so mustn't grumble!

Write soon!

DEAD SKIN

Pilla.

117

Dear Cara,
A terrible day! And it started **DRIBBLE!** so well - the cat slept on the pillow and left delicious globs of dried spit for our breakfast! The interesting fishy flavour makes a change from all that dead skin! Anyway, I puffed out a bit of gas **PUFF** from my bum (no it wasn't a fart, silly, it was a chemical signal to the family to come and eat) and I saw the huge jaws...

A cheyletus. I don't have to tell you what these bugs do to us dust mites! It was after me but I got away. It grabbed my little sister and gobbled her up! I always used to argue with my sister but she went down a treat with the monster. Well, if I can't be safe in my own bed where can I be safe? I've crawled into the human's clothes and when the human gets into them I'm off to seek my fortune.
See you on the carpet.
Your mite,   Pilla   **BYE!**

☠ HORRIBLE HEALTH WARNING!

Pillow mites don't do any harm and if you make a fuss about going to bed you'll probably be given a block of wood for a pillow. Oh well, you'll sleep like a log!

Mind you, there are more mites in your home than you mite think. There's a *mitey* BIG number ... just take a look at this:

And that's not all... Not surprisingly, your house is *bulging* with bacteria. They're oozing over the furniture and slurping into the wallpaper and in the kitchen they're slobbering and squelching in your food. Dinner anyone?

THE MICROBE
GOOD FOOD GUIDE...
By Mike Robe

Hi micro-munchers! There's nothing that we bacteria like better than a little nibble of nosh but we all suffer little dinner-time disasters. I'll never forget the day I tried to eat disinfectant! Anyway, here's our guide to the smartest and cheapest places to eat out as sampled by our team of inspectors — the slime squad!

A word about safety...

Safety is very important. Every year billions of bacteria suffer fatal accidents which could have been prevented by a little safety awareness. Things to beware of when eating out...

1 BLEACH Run a mile – and if you can't manage a mile, you'd better squirm a few millimetres. **BLEACH WILL KILL YOU INSTANTLY!**

2 SALT Don't eat too much of this. You'll find that your body will suck in water to dilute the salt and you'll explode!

THE KITCHEN BIN BISTRO

The classic eatery! A must for all gourmet bacteria. Easily the most wide-ranging menu, plus old favourites such as "cat food and cold mashed potato cottage pie" and "dad's cooking's gone wrong again" and that all-time favourite "last night's leftover curry". For pudding why not try slimy yoghurt scum? Recommended!

A cheap and cheerful watering hole with a smelly atmosphere all of its own. Here you can relax in the moist surroundings and dine on a delightful range of dishes including mouldy breadcrumb surprise and greasy fat soup.

THE DISHCLOTH DINER

THE COLD STEW CAFÉ

Delicious boiled meat and vegetables proved easy to digest with just a sprinkling of salt (but thankfully not enough to spoil the taste). There were delicious and tempting extras on offer such as "fresh fungi and mite-poo pudding". No wonder the restaurant was packed with bacteria! Recommended!

THE TIN CAN HOTEL
(guests only)

No bacteria are allowed past the strong metal walls! Conditions inside are said to be grim with no atmosphere at all! Actually we found out that bacteria do eat there but they're guests and sometimes they trash the place and cause nasty stinks.

~SCIENTIFIC NOTE~
These bacteria don't need oxygen to live.

The chemicals on the staff were a really hard-boiled lot and made us feel unwelcome – and that's no yolk – er, joke. One of our team was so badly treated that she dissolved! Best avoided.

THE GOLDEN EGG

~SCIENTIFIC NOTE~
Eggs contain chemicals that dissolve bacteria.

I'm afraid this was another eatery that didn't live up to its initial promise. Although there was delicious fat on the menu the service was rather cold and eventually we felt we were being frozen out.

THE ICE-CREAM PARLOUR

Now you've had your meal, how about ruining your teacher's lunch?

This may not be very wise. If you get expelled for doing this you don't know me, OK?

The HORRIBLE SCIENCE guide to

PUTTING TEACHERS OFF THEIR LUNCH

Step one – Make sure you sit at the same table as your teacher. Bellowing these facts across the canteen could get you into even worse trouble.

Step two – During the meal it's important to make sure that your table manners are perfect.

Things not to do...**DO NOT** pick your nose. **DO NOT** eat with your mouth open or smack your lips. **DO NOT** burp and wipe your greasy mouth on your sleeve...good luck!

Rotten taste? Did you know that the taste of that chicken is mostly due to the bacteria that are crawling over the dead meat?

The mashed potato should be OK.

Dud spud, you mean. Under a microscope you can see how boiling the potato has broken open its box-like cells. This makes it easier for bacteria to feed on the food inside. Chances are it's crawling with germs!

I need a glass of water!

Has this glass been washed properly? If not it might contain a tiny amoeba that dribbled out of the mouth of the last person to drink from it. If you drink from the glass the amoeba will slop into your mouth and make itself at home.

Where's the bathroom?

Bet you never knew!
If you looked at milk under a powerful microscope it wouldn't be white! The white colour comes from blobs of a chemical called casein that contains proteins. The casein reflects the light to give a white colour. But the rest of the liquid is clear water with blobs of yellow fat and smaller chemicals and minerals bobbing about in the milk. Hope you've got enough bottle to drink it!

Teacher's tea-break teaser

Try this one and you'll be as welcome as a woodworm in a wooden leg factory ... so don't forget to SMILE.

Pound your fists on the staffroom door. When it opens your teacher will be desperately clutching a well-earned cup of tea. Ask them:

Answer:
When you boil a kettle there are bound to be bacteria in the water. They may have got into the kettle from the air or they may have been in the water. As the water heats up the bacteria will start to feel warm and comfy. But the growing heat will burn their tiny hairs and melt their slimy bodies. This is a very cruel fate even for bacteria. How can your teacher stomach drinking tea flavoured with murdered melted germs?

Mind you, if this talk of slimy bacteria has you dashing to the toilet I've got bad news. The bacteria have got there first and you're about to encounter THE ULTIMATE HORROR!

Dare you face...

TERROR IN THE TOILET

GRRR!

If bacteria are getting under your skin or on your skin or up your nose or anywhere else, what should you do?

a) Pick your nose and spots.

b) Get someone else to pick your nose and spots.

c) Wash the bacteria off.

Answer:

c) Probably – or as a scientist would say ..."yes" and "no". Let's face a few facts before reaching for that bar of soap...

Microscopic monsters fact file

NAME: Washing and germs

1 Most people think that soap kills germs, but in fact most people are wrong. Soap doesn't usually kill germs, but it does send them on a one-way trip to the sewer. Here's how...

ARGH!

2 Washing your hands in water won't get rid of germs because they cling to the greasy surface of the skin. The water and grease don't mix so nothing happens.

CLING!

GERMS

GREASE

3 Tiny bits of soap (scientists call them molecules) consist of a "head" containing sodium and a "tail" made of chemicals called hydrocarbons (hi-dro-car-bons).

This allows the water to wash grease, soap and germs down the plug hole!

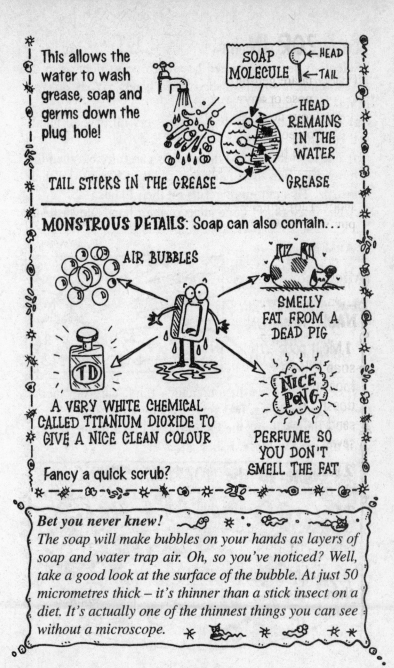

SOAP MOLECULE ← HEAD ← TAIL

HEAD REMAINS IN THE WATER

TAIL STICKS IN THE GREASE

GREASE

MONSTROUS DETAILS: Soap can also contain...

AIR BUBBLES

SMELLY FAT FROM A DEAD PIG

A VERY WHITE CHEMICAL CALLED TITANIUM DIOXIDE TO GIVE A NICE CLEAN COLOUR

NICE PONG

PERFUME SO YOU DON'T SMELL THE FAT

Fancy a quick scrub?

Bet you never knew!
The soap will make bubbles on your hands as layers of soap and water trap air. Oh, so you've noticed? Well, take a good look at the surface of the bubble. At just 50 micrometres thick – it's thinner than a stick insect on a diet. It's actually one of the thinnest things you can see without a microscope.

Could you be a scientist?

Scientists secretly studied how a group of doctors in an Australian hospital washed their hands. What do you think they found?

a) The doctors carefully washed every bit of their hands to get rid of any germs.

b) The doctors washed their hands carefully but then did things like bite their nails and plucked hairs from their nostrils. This put more germs on their hands.

c) The doctors left large areas of their hands unwashed.

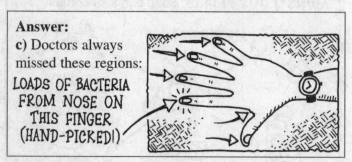

Answer:

c) Doctors always missed these regions:

LOADS OF BACTERIA FROM NOSE ON THIS FINGER (HAND-PICKED!)

Next time you wash your hands think carefully about what you're doing. Did you miss any vital bits?

Not surprisingly, the bathroom is like a nature reserve for microbe wildlife. Fancy a tour?

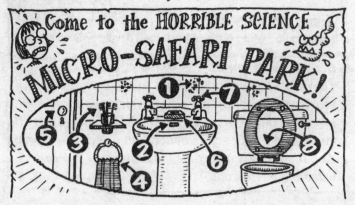

Come to the HORRIBLE SCIENCE MICRO-SAFARI PARK!

Lots of fun for all the family... in fact it's so much fun you won't be able to get them out of the bathroom even when you want to go to the toilet!

❶ EXPLORE THE EXCITING BLACK MOULD FOREST!

The black spots you can see are actually the structures that make spores to make more black moulds whilst the little feeding tubes underneath eat your bathroom!

OOER!

❷ GO SCUBA DIVING in the romantic sink overflow — it's the place in the bathroom which has more germs than any other!

❸ CLIMB THE TOOTHBRUSH!

It's crawling with germs — if you're lucky you'll spot a mouth-amoeba eating the bacteria!

CHOMP!

❹ EXPLORE THE TOWELS for stray dust mites and demodex creatures.

MUNCH!

❺ THE DOOR KNOB is a wonderful place to spot germs especially after someone's had a poo and not washed their hands properly. (One in five toilet door knobs have tiny lumps of poo on.)

PHWOAR!

6 FEEDING TIME AT THE SOAP BAR. If it's wet you should see lots of germs happily eating the soap!

CHEW!

7 Round off your visit with a trip to the taps to be entertained by the amazing TAP-DANCING BACTERIA!

TAP! "TAP!
TAP! TAP!

8 Grand Finale: Marvel at the TOILET FLUSH-FOUNTAIN as it showers you with tiny droplets of water and pee and germs and lumps of poo...

PLOP!

FLUSH!

Smellie School
Greater Whiffing
Dear Sir,
I would like to complain about your book where it says that toilets spray germs and other unmentionable matter. As a result of your book no one's dared to flush the toilets in our school for six weeks and the situation is getting desperate. Excuse me as I adjust my clothes-peg on my nose. This time you've really gone too far! It's not even true ... is it?
Yours crossly,
  Mrs Head (Head)

Well Mrs Head, I'M AFRAID IT'S TRUE...

Admittedly the droplets are too small to see – a few micrometres across. But just for you, Mrs Head, here's an experiment designed to make them visible. We've recruited fearless private eye MI Gutzache to flush this toilet.

The water has been stained with a brown dye and when you turn the lights off the dye glows in the dark. Mind you, the toilet hasn't been cleaned for a few months so we hope that brown stuff in the water is just the dye. We've also rigged up a high-speed camera with special high-speed film capable of photographing microscopic droplets flying about in the dark...

Oh well, now for the moment of truth!

The deadly exploding toilet experiment

131

You can see a cloud of 10 billion shining droplets rising up from the toilet bowl like a giant sneeze. Normally these are too small to see, which is why you can't see them when you flush.

The droplets engulf Gutzache

Gutzache is covered in the glistening substance.

THERE AIN'T NOTHING TO IT!

• SCIENTIFIC NOTE •
Laboratory analysis reveals that these droplets contain bacteria, viruses, poo and pee. Let's hope Gutzache doesn't read this bit!

A quick note to the reader...
Scared yet?
1 DON'T try flushing the chain with the lid down. Apparently this makes the cloud of droplets and germs worse because it squirts out under the lid with greater force.
2 DO flush the chain yourself – no, don't bribe your little brother/sister to do it or leave you-know-whats bobbing about in the loo. And don't be scared! Your body fights off the germs.

And whilst we're on the toilet – I mean on the *subject* of the toilet – here are some facts that you definitely shouldn't read aloud at mealtimes...

Eight microscopic facts that you always wanted to know about toilets and never dared ask...

- Public toilet urinals (the things that men pee in) often spray back microscopic drops of pee on to shoes and trousers. This can be a wee bit embarrassing.

- The nasty sharp smell in dirty public toilets is probably ammonia. This is a chemical produced by bacteria which they make by eating another chemical found in pee called urea. You might be interested to know that ammonia is great for growing plants but when babies get it on their skin it causes nappy rash.

- In Roman times the ammonia from pee was used to make mouthwash and toothpaste. Fancy a gargle?

WE RAN OUT OF PEE SO I MADE THIS BATCH FROM POO

CHOKE!

- In some places in the USA toilet seats are covered in disposable paper to protect your bum from germs. Actually there aren't that many germs on toilet seats. Maybe they get squashed when people with large bottoms sit on them.
- Are you keen on saving paper? One of the cleanest toilets in the world is a Japanese invention that sprays your bum with water and dries it with hot air so you don't need any toilet paper. It even sprays scent on your bum to give it a nice fresh smell.
- Alternatively, if you really want to look after the environment why not buy a compost loo? There's lots of versions available. On one Dutch invention you can rock back and forward whilst you sit on the toilet. (You might as well take a radio in and listen to rock and roll music while you're at it.) The rocking motion mixes the poo with soil inside the toilet. Within a few weeks germs rot the poo into lovely fertiliser for the garden!

WHAT A BEAUTIFUL GARDEN. YOU MUST HAVE GREEN FINGERS!

THEY'RE BROWN, ACTUALLY!

- Much of the nasty smell in farts is from chemicals made by germs that live in the gut. Oh, so you knew that? Well, did you know that farting *killed* one man? Simon Tup was a Victorian entertainer – well, it's entertainment if you like that kind of thing. His act was called "the farting blacksmith" and he used to fart in time to music. Sadly, one night Simon's version of "Blow high and blow low" proved too much. He burst a blood vessel and died for his fart ... er, I mean art.

- One night in 1856 Matthew Gladman went to the toilet in his home town of Lewes, England. Unfortunately the floor of the toilet had been removed prior to cleaning the pit underneath. Down Matthew fell into a deep pit of doo-doo ... Gladman wasn't a glad man! He died of suffocation by methane gas from the germs as they fed on the rotting poo.

Of course, things have improved since those days. Nowadays your school toilets are not placed above a deep pit full of poo (and children are no longer thrown in when they're naughty). Chances are they're connected up to a sewage works. And when it comes to getting rid of big jobs the tiny microbes have a BIG JOB!

Bet you never knew!
At sewage works sewage is rotted down by a range of bacteria that eat the poo and paper. OK, so you knew that? Well, did you know that scientists have found that bacteria in sewage are very good at making vitamin B12, a chemical that helps build healthy nerve cells. In fact, if you take a vitamin supplement the B12 may have been made by these bacteria!

Actually, this is just one of many discoveries made as scientists learn more about the microscopic world. But what are these discoveries and where are they taking us? Is small really going to be beautiful or are we heading for a GINORMOUS monster disaster?

Time to leave this chapter and start the next page...

WASH YOUR HANDS FIRST!

EPILOGUE: IT'S A SMALL, SMALL, SMALL, SMALL WORLD

Some people think BIG. Big plans, big ideas, big money and they often have big heads to match. Other people think small and amongst them are many scientists who believe that microscopic technology holds the tiny little key to our future...

But will these plans work out...?

Well, the only way to be sure is to go and see and that means time travel into the future. As luck would have it, Professor N Large has been working on a time machine and the obvious person to test it is fearless investigator MI Gutzache...

Oh all right, maybe we'll have to experiment on an animal. Perhaps Tiddles can be coaxed into trying it...

I am keen to discover the future direction of micro-research. I've written a letter to future scientists to introduce Tiddles and fitted her with a video camera to record her experiences in the year 2050.

Dear Future Colleague,
This is to introduce my cat Tiddles who I have sent into the future to test my time-machine and return with a record of micro-technology in your time. Please help her with the video controls and send her back in one piece.
Thanks a lot,
Prof. N. Large

ARE YOU READY TIDDLES?

Dear Prof. N. Large
Thanks for your letter. We couldn't work out how to work that funny old-fashioned video camera. Anyway, we sorted it out in the end.
Prof. I.B Smalle

And here's the video Tiddles brought back...

Hi Prof. Things are great in 2050! Thanks to micro-technology, we've solved the world food problem! Everyone now eats chlorella algae — you can grow it much faster than any other food. It tastes like spinach but hey — you get used to it!

Anyway, you can genetically engineer it to look and taste like anything — even cat food!

ALGAE CAT

SCIENTIFIC NOTE...

Genetic engineering involves adding new bits to the DNA of bacteria. The new DNA programs the microbes to make any protein chemical you like. One example is human growth-hormone. (Oddly enough, that's the substance that makes people grow.) In the past people who couldn't make enough were treated with injections of the stuff taken from dead bodies. Now back to the future...

And now, thanks to genetic engineering, we grow elastin — as you know that's the stretchy substance in your body found around joints and elsewhere. Anyway, its great for making bandages and new blood vessels!

And right now genetically engineered bacteria are being produced for space travel! They eat astronauts' poo and pee and turn it into delicious snack bars which they can eat again! Yum yum!

And micro-technology is BIG BUSINESS NOW. My favourite game is nanofootball. You use a nanomanipulator — a super-powerful virtual reality electron-microscope with 3D graphics that makes you feel you're kicking atoms about! It's cool!

Mind you, these nanomanipulators aren't toys. We use them all the time to make tiny nanomachines! When I'm out and about, I use the computer embedded in my fingernail. I wouldn't leave home without it and it's stopped me biting my nails!

There are nanomachines in my clothes that make them change colour whenever I feel like it!

SORRY READERS, YOU'LL HAVE TO IMAGINE THE COLOURS.

And there are nanomachines inside my body at the moment killing germs! Oh well, your cat doesn't like microbe cat food so I'm sending her back! Bye for now!

So you don't believe a word of all this?

Well ... it's based on FACT *because the future is already happening*!

1 Scientists have already suggested chlorella algae as a future food source.

2 Biotechnology was developed in the 1980s and 1990s. In 1996 scientists made bacteria that made elastin-type substances.

3 It's possible to make the bacteria that recycle human waste into food using genetic engineering.

4 Nanomanipulators really exist! They were developed in American university labs in the later 1990s.

5 As for the nanomachines, they don't exist ... yet. But they've made a small beginning! Here's some simple stuff that's been around long enough to reach the shops...

TINY TREATS

Welcome to the world's smallest shop. It fits into a thimble! The kids will love it! (If they can find it.)

LOOKING FOR THAT LITTLE SOMETHING FOR CHRISTMAS?

The world's smallest powered toy car was made by Toyota in 1997. At just 5 mm (0.2 inches) long you'll have no problem parking! Travels 1.6 km (one mile) a day.

The very small print: Needs battery and wire.

ER, CHEERS

LITTLE TIME TO SPARE?

You need the world's smallest watch. Each gear is thinner than a hair!

WATCH!

I AM WATCHING BUT I STILL CAN'T SEE IT!

The very small print: Your watch can only count seconds. Anyway, if it had hands you wouldn't be able to see them.

FANCY A LITTLE MUSIC?

I GIVE UP!

PLUCK!

You will with this cool six-string guitar made at Cornell University in 1996. Made out of silicon atoms, it's the size of a human cell. All your concerts will be cell-outs!

The very small print: You may have trouble playing your guitar because it's millions of times smaller than your fingers and the strings don't twang.

NEED A LITTLE MATHS HELP?

Solve maths problems with an atom abacus! You move the atoms along tiny grooves and it helps you do sums. Get every answer right without your teacher even realizing it's there!

WHAT ARE YOU UP TO, JENKINS?

The very small print: Hopefully, your teacher won't notice you're using a giant electron microscope to operate your abacus.

OK, these inventions could do with a tiny bit of improvement. So is the future really full of BIG POSSIBILITIES or are scientists just being small-minded? Well, come what may – the future's bound to hold a few little surprises. But at least you can be sure of one thing: this book has been about the horrible world of the really, really tiny – the world that you can see through a microscope. But once you've peered down that eyepiece and glimpsed this strange place the outside world that you see every day will never seem the same again...

Oh well, that's Horrible Science for you!

THE END

DEADLY DISEASES

INTRODUCTION

Are you well?

If so, GREAT. If not, maybe you need the *Horrible Science* treatment! Take one copy of this book and read it in large doses – after food. (Reading it before meals can ruin your appetite.) You're bound to feel better because laughter is a great healer!

(AND THAT'S JUST THE CONTENTS PAGE)

And if you're not ill you ought to read this book anyway to maintain a healthy sense of humour.

This book is especially effective against SLUMP disease (that's Science Lessons Upset Mystified Pupils). Sufferers of this common condition often slump over desks and feel a strong urge to sleep. And sadly, SLUMP disease can prove deadly ... deadly boring, that is.

INFECTIOUS PATHOGENS, BLAH BLAH, MUMBLE, DRONE.

I'M BORED

I'M DEAD BORED

I'M DEAD

Well, if you're a SLUMP sufferer, cheer up! This book contains medically proven ingredients such as sick jokes and sickening stories and seriously sick facts to fight SLUMP disease by boosting your brain power. This treatment is so successful that afterwards you can test your teacher and dumbfound your doctor with your deadly disease discoveries! Read about fiendishly foul phenomena like the nurse who drank diarrhoea...

and the scientist who died of the disease he was studying...

and the doctors who *killed* one another because they argued over a disease.

Feeling better yet? You will soon. Just keep on reading! But be warned...

WARNING!

SIDE EFFECTS OF THIS BOOK CAN INCLUDE SNORTS OF LAUGHTER AT EMBARRASSING MOMENTS, AND FEELING AN URGE TO TRY REVOLTING EXPERIMENTS.

Well, what are you waiting for...?

THE SICKENING FACTS

DISEASES COULD WIPE OUT THE HUMAN RACE!

It sounds sickening – but is it a fact? Well, you can check on your survival chances later on, but now it's time for a story to get your brain juices going...

The invasion

The aliens landed on a Saturday at about 7.30 pm.

Alex and his parents were having tea when they arrived. Huge dark green shapes loomed at the windows, lumbering like bears. There was a crash as an alien vaporized the door with its heat gun. It had two staring eyes like a giant squid and tentacles around its mouth.

"ARGGGH!" screamed Alex.

"Blimey!" said his dad.

"Hello vicar," said his mum, searching for her glasses.

"Ulla ulla ulla!" said the alien, opening its razor-sharp fangs.

All three humans turned to run. There was a whooshing sound followed by a nasty burning smell as one of the aliens microwaved the cat.

Within hours the army had sealed off the area. The roads were clogged with people trying to flee. Everyone was unsure where to go, everyone was scared. It was worse than the first day at a new school.

"Don't panic!" shouted the general through a battered army megaphone. "We'll stop them!"

Just then a red haze appeared glowing against the sky. It was a cloud of gas billowing and tumbling like thick smoke. Ahead of the gas, soldiers from an advance patrol came running and stumbling and choking and falling.

"Gas masks!" ordered the general.

"Er ... sorry, sir, we left them at the base!" stammered his sergeant.

"Then we'll have to make a rapid strategic withdrawal!" barked the general.

"Come again, sir?" asked the sergeant.

The general swung round bellowing "THAT MEANS RUN, YOU BLITHERING IDIOT!"

Soon the whole country was in uproar. All the roads were jammed with cars trying to escape the gas that hung in little wisps and unexpectedly seeped under doors. There was no TV because the aliens had knocked out the electricity system, but at least the schools were closed. Alex and his parents found themselves hiding in a sewer.

"I need some fresh air!" gasped Alex as he clambered towards the entrance.

"This subway needs a good clean," said his mum (who still hadn't found her glasses).

"You'll need more than fresh air if the gas gets you!" warned his dad, but the boy wasn't listening.

Alex sniffed the air. It seemed fresh enough. Well, it would after the sewer. So he decided it was safe to look for food and crept cautiously down the road. Suddenly he froze – an alien patrol had appeared round the corner! There was nowhere to hide. Alex closed his eyes and waited to be microwaved.

But the aliens ignored him.

They stumbled and shuffled past saying something like...

"Ulla, urgle, gurgle!"

Thick orange dribble slobbered from their mouths and their tentacles were droopy.

Taking courage, Alex followed the aliens into a field where he saw an awesome sight. Several spacecraft were leaning at drunken angles. All around lay aliens, many dead but a few twitching. There was a vile smell like rotting school-dinner cabbage.

The boy couldn't believe his eyes.

The aliens were sick, they were being destroyed.

But how and why?

Just then an alien sneezed a big glob of purple snot. Alex realized that the aliens had the most appalling, stinking colds. The invaders hadn't been defeated by the army or by anything that humans could do. No, they were beaten by humble common-or-garden germs.

Cool story?! It was inspired by a novel, *War of the Worlds* by H.G. Wells (1866-1946), in which diseases halt an alien invasion. Bet you never knew that hovering over every 6.4 square cm (one square inch) of ground there are 4,000 microbes looking for somewhere to land, someone to attack. And if you live in a big city there'll be about 400,000 germs hovering over your head! It's enough to make your hair curl.

No wonder the aliens never stood a chance!

So what about us? Are we going to be wiped out like the aliens? Well, germs certainly give us a tough time – you can be *dead* sure of that. But before we delve into their murky world – here's a chance to check your existing knowledge.

Odd diseases quiz

1 Which of these animals does NOT get colds?
a) Teachers.
b) Ferrets.
c) Fish.

2 Which of the following animals does NOT get flu?
a) Pigs.
b) Ducks.
c) Woodlice.

3 Which of the following treatments is USELESS against germs?
a) Feeding a maggot on diseased flesh.
b) Smearing a wound with honey.
c) Plonking a dollop of bat's poo on a wound.

4 Where will you NEVER find germs?
a) The moon.
b) Mars (that's the planet not the choccie bar).
c) A school dinner.

5 Which substance is USELESS for killing germs?
a) Moon dust.
b) Custard.
c) Toilet cleaner.

Answers:

1 c) If fish got colds their paper hankies would go soggy.

You may be interested to know that in the 1930s a scientist discovered that ferrets get colds after a ferret sneezed on him and he developed the illness.

2 c) Ever seen a woodlouse sipping lemsip?

In fact, you can catch flu from pigs and even ducks (that's when you need a quack doctor!). You can breathe these germs in or, even worse, the germs pass out of the animals' faeces (poo) into water. If humans drink the water we fall ill too. Sickening, eh?

3 c) The poo is crawling with germs. Doctors in Washington DC, in the USA, covered an injured girl's germ-infected leg with 1,500 maggots. The maggots ate the germs and diseased flesh but left the healthy bits. Honey is great for killing germs – the sugary stuff dries them out. That's why honey keeps for months in a cupboard after you've opened it. Mind you, if you want to keep your family sweet don't go smearing their honey on your scabby wounds and then putting the knife back in the pot.

4 b) Scientists tested Martian soil for germs in 1977 and found none. School dinners are full of germs and scientists have even found germs on the moon! In the 1970s astronauts brought back a piece of an old lunar-landing vehicle left on the moon in 1967. Inside the protective casing of the vehicle's camera, the scientists found germs from snot that had got into material when it was made. *The germs were still alive!*

5 b) Germs happily scoff custard. Toilet cleaner contains bleach, a highly effective germ-killer. And scientists in Houston, USA, have found that moon dust actually contains chemicals that kill germs – trouble is your local chemist probably doesn't sell moon dust and if they did it would cost £5 million a gram!

A NOTE TO THE READER

This is a little book about a big subject. There are thousands of different diseases. There are nasty diseases, smelly diseases and diseases you can't even tell your mum about. Some are caused by poisonous chemicals and others by worms in the guts. To fit them all in a book you'd need a book the size of a bookcase. So to save space, this book deals only with the deadly diseases caused by tiny living things – microbes.

DON'T WORRY, IT'S NOT CAUSED BY MICROBES...

...JUST WORMS IN YOUR GUTS

So how are you feeling now? Maybe a bit shivery, or perhaps a bit sick? Perhaps these germs might be doing something nasty to *you*? Could it be that you've already got one of the deadly diseases we'll be looking at in this book?!

SHIVER!

SHAKE!

SWEAT!

TREMBLE!

We've hired Dr Grimgrave – the most miserable doctor in the world (he really ought to read a *Horrible Science* book to cheer himself up!) – to tell you the worst...

DR GRIMGRAVE'S GUIDE TO SYMPTOMS

So how are we today? Deadly disease, eh? Well, I'll need to examine you ... do you have any of these symptoms? If you aren't sure, I can arrange a consultation but not for idiots and time-wasters. Being a doctor could be enjoyable if it wasn't for all those whinging, sick people one has to see.

VIOLENT COUGH

Coughing is normal. I encourage my patients to cough into a handkerchief because it's the body's way of removing mucus

OFTEN A LOVELY GREEN COLOUR

(snot) caused by an infection. A violent cough, fever and huge lumps under the armpits and black spots on the skin may be a sign of one form of plague. Rapid burial in earth may be the most effective treatment here.

Dear reader
We apologise for the poor quality jokes. Dr Grimgrave is not known for his sense of humour.

DEADLY DIARRHOEA

ESSENTIAL
EQUIPMENT

Severe diarrhoea turns from brown to green and becomes paler when it contains the gut lining. This could be a sign of cholera. If untreated, there is continuous diarrhoea until the victim's body dries out. My old colleague, Dr Twinge caught cholera and he nearly dried of it.

SOMETIMES
LOOKS LIKE
BIGPOX,
HA HA!

PUS-FILLED PUSTULES

Spots are caused by minor infections resulting in a build-up of pus. Violent fever, muscle pains and spots filled with pus covering most of the upper body were a symptom of smallpox. In severe cases large chunks of flesh die and fall off the victim's body – most unhygienic.

DANGEROUS DRIBBLING

IT'S A
MOUTH-WATERING
EXPERIENCE!

Uncontrollable salivation can be a symptom of rabies. Other signs include fear of water, and an inability to swallow. By the time the disease reaches this stage there is no cure. Honestly, what do these patients expect me to do ... heal them?

BRIGHT YELLOW SKIN

The liver fails and chemicals escape and build up under the skin — jaundice, we doctors call it.

(I always think that if the liver is bad you should try onions — they improve the taste no end. Ha ha.) Jaundice and black vomit are signs of yellow fever. I have a sample of this remarkable regurgitation in my private medical collection.

FEEL LIKE DEATH AND *LOOK* LIKE A BANANA!

PLEASE NOTE: you're unlikely to have these deadly diseases. Most mild diseases can be treated by taking a painkiller and going to bed and allowing the body to heal itself. That way you don't bother me, your doctor. Now, if you'll excuse me, I've got work to do...

We'll be getting to grips with the gore and pus later on, but first a question: what actually *causes* all these deadly diseases? Yep, I'm sorry, but it's time to look at some deadly disease germs, and you can catch them in the next chapter...

GRUESOME GERMS

Take a peek down this microscope and you'll see them...

WE USED TO LIVE IN A LOVELY WARM NOSE...

...BUT A SCIENTIST "PICKED" US FOR HIS RESEARCH

Not much to look at, maybe, but they're the nastiest and deadliest killers the human race has ever known. Just take a look at their files...

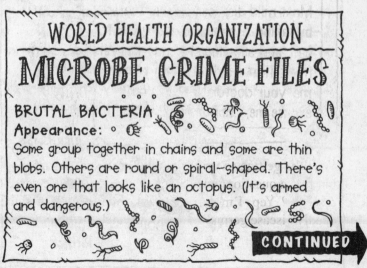

WORLD HEALTH ORGANIZATION
MICROBE CRIME FILES

BRUTAL BACTERIA
Appearance:
Some group together in chains and some are thin blobs. Others are round or spiral-shaped. There's even one that looks like an octopus. (It's armed and dangerous.)

CONTINUED

163

Size:

Most bacteria are 0.5 – 1.5 micrometres in size. (Up to 10,000 bacteria can stretch across your thumbnail – you'd better wash your hands afterwards!)

Horrible places they live:

Everywhere! Bacteria particularly like dirty places, like sewers or mounds of poo. Millions live in your guts (where they do no harm except make chemicals that make farts smelly).

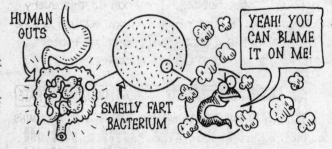

HUMAN GUTS

SMELLY FART BACTERIUM

YEAH! YOU CAN BLAME IT ON ME!

Favourite food:

They're not fussy. In fact, they even eat school dinners! They particularly like bits of dead or live body if they can get inside the skin. And many bacteria love human blood with its comforting warmth and delicious gloopy sugar snacks. (Luckily for the germs, there isn't *too* much sugar in blood, unlike honey!)

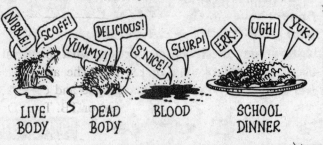

NIBBLE! SCOFF! YUMMY! DELICIOUS! S'NICE! SLURP! ERK! UGH! YUK!

LIVE BODY   DEAD BODY   BLOOD   SCHOOL DINNER

Nasty habits:

Make deadly chemicals called toxins (tock-sins) that can stop human nerves working so the person can't move. The toxins kill by stopping the victim's breathing or disrupting their heartbeat. These bacteria are heart-less!

Brutal behaviour:

If they're warm and well-fed, bacteria happily increase in numbers by splitting in half. (Yeah – they're split personalities.) They can do this every 20 minutes, so in just nine hours one bacterium (one of these things is a bacterium, two or more are *bacteria*) can produce 100 million copies.

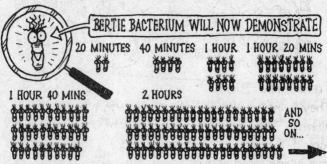

BERTIE BACTERIUM WILL NOW DEMONSTRATE

20 MINUTES 40 MINUTES 1 HOUR 1 HOUR 20 MINS

1 HOUR 40 MINS 2 HOURS AND SO ON...

If they do this inside the body they make huge slimy lumps that break up the body's vital organs and cause death. Yikes!

Terrible TB

By now you might be wondering what bacterial diseases are lurking in wait for you. The answer is *plenty*. For example, besides the plague and cholera, there's tuberculosis (ter-burk-u-lo-sis) or TB. Trust Dr Grimgrave to break the news gently...

HEALTH NEWS

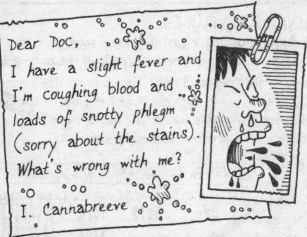

Dear Doc,

I have a slight fever and I'm coughing blood and loads of snotty phlegm (sorry about the stains). What's wrong with me?

I. Cannabreeve

Dear Mr Cannabreeve, My hobby happens to be breeding bacteria and judging by the ones I found in the stains on the letter — you have TB.

I'm sorry to say that this lung disease is the biggest killer in the world but a course of drugs called antibiotics should save you.*
PS Don't call me Doc.

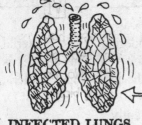

INFECTED LUNGS

Your body is trying to clear your lungs of the Tuberculosis bacteria.

ANTI BIOTICS

* For more information on antibiotics see page 212.

Mind you, if you think that sounds bad – just wait until you see the next section of the MICROBE CRIME FILES.

MICROBE CRIME FILES – PART 2

VICIOUS VIRUSES

Appearance: Weird-looking – some are like lunar landing craft and others look like anti-ship mines covered in spikes.

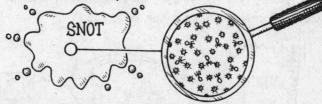

SNOT

Size: 17 to 300 nanometres. You could fit a chain of ten *million* viruses across your thumbnail (though you'll need a steady hand and a lot of patience).

ANTI-SHIP MINE

DEADLY

DEADLIER

VIRUS

Horrible places they live: Viruses have no proper bodies to protect them from heat or cold and that's why they live inside cells. (No, not *police* cells, silly, I mean the tiny living blobs of jelly that make up our bodies.)

Favourite food: Viruses don't eat or breathe. In fact, some scientists reckon they're not even alive! Think of viruses as vampires – creatures neither dead nor alive that prey on unsuspecting humans. No wonder they're a pain in the neck!

Nasty habits: The virus sticks to a cell and hijacks the control system of the cell and forces it to make copies of the virus. When the cell is worn out it dies and the viruses go in search of another victim. (For more details see page 255.)

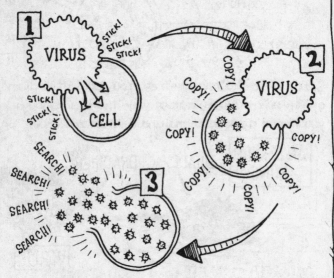

Vicious behaviour: Viruses often spread in tiny drops of spit that spray out of the mouth when we cough or sneeze. This danger is not to be sniffed at. Here are some interesting notes that I wrote on my hankie...

SNOTTY SNEEZY FACTS

1 One sneeze can contain *six million* viruses! Next time a cold makes you sneeze try counting them!

2 Millions of microscopic snot lumps shoot out of your nose and mouth at 64 km (40 miles) per hour. If your sneeze was a gust of wind it would be strong enough to snap twigs off trees!

3 Within seconds the water in the snot dries out encasing the germs in hard dry snot like tiny bullets (but too light for anyone to feel). If someone's in the way some snot might go down their throat or up their nose and some might go on their hands and they might then put their fingers in their mouth. And that's how your germs get into someone else.

WOULD YOU LIKE TO BORROW MY HANKIE?

NO THANKS!

MICROBE CRIME FILES - PART 3

REVOLTING IN-BETWEENIES

No, that isn't their scientific name. These are actually living things that are smaller than bacteria and bigger than viruses – the best known are rickettsia (rick-ket-see-a).

CONTINUED ➡

Appearance: Tiny blobs of colourless jelly.

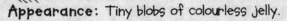

Size: 0.5 micrometres across. You could fit 20,000 in a line across your thumbnail. (Now where did you put those viruses?)

NOW YOU KNOW WHY MUM SAYS, "DON'T PICK YOUR NOSE!"

Horrible places they live: Rickettsia live inside insects like ticks and lice. Typhus rickettsia live inside blood-sucking lice that lurk on unwashed bodies. Maybe that's why they spread lousy diseases? The germs emerge in lice poo or eggs which enter the human body through the skin when it is scratched.

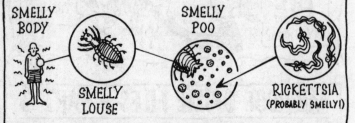

SMELLY BODY

SMELLY POO

SMELLY LOUSE

RICKETTSIA (PROBABLY SMELLY!)

Because the rickettsia are so small they can hide inside body cells and this makes them hard to find.

Nasty habits: Typhus rickettsia cause the disease typhus fever.

So what is typhus fever?
Dr Grimgrave knows the dreadful details...

HEALTH NEWS

SICK? NEED ADVICE?
Write to Dr Grimgrave and if he's not too busy he might bother to reply to your questions...

Dear Dr Grimgrave,
The day before yesterday I had backache. Now I've got a splitting headache, fever and I think I'm starting with a rash. I can't sleep. Am I going to die?

Yours,   Vera Sicke

Dear Ms Sicke,
Yes, probably. You have typhus and you may die of heart failure caused by germ toxins. But the rash might turn to sores which might rot and if your fingers and toes are infected they might drop off. If so, could you spare them for my private medical collection?

If you want to get better, I'd recommend antibiotics, which should stop the disease developing.

Now if you'll excuse me, my patients are getting impatient.

> IF YOU CAN'T SLEEP TRY LYING ON THE EDGE OF THE BED ~ YOU'LL SOON DROP OFF

> IF YOU COULD SPARE FIVE FINGERS, THAT WOULD *REALLY* BE GIVING ME A HAND

Now back to those files...

MICROBE CRIME FILES - PART 4

PUTRID PROTOZOA

Appearance: Blobs of colourless jelly. Protozoa look a bit like human cells and that makes them rather hard to spot inside the body. Imagine trying to find a toffee in a chocolate factory.

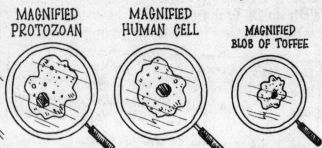

MAGNIFIED PROTOZOAN

MAGNIFIED HUMAN CELL

MAGNIFIED BLOB OF TOFFEE

Size: Most are less than 0.5 millimetres across. (So you'd need at least 20 big-uns to stretch across that grubby thumbnail.)

GET LOST RICKETTSIA!

NO WAY! WE WERE HERE FIRST

Horrible places they live: Often make themselves at home inside other creatures – in places such as guts or blood where they cause disease by making toxins.

I FEEL SICK – THINK I'M GONNA DIE.

HOW DO YOU KNOW?

IT'S JUST A GUT FEELING

Nasty habits: It depends on the disease. Take malaria for example – this disease is caused by protozoa with as much conscience as a gang of piranhas in a goldfish bowl.

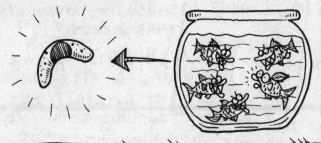

NAME: Malaria

THE BASIC FACTS:

1 The protozoa are spread by Anopheles (a-noff-fa-lees) mosquitoes.

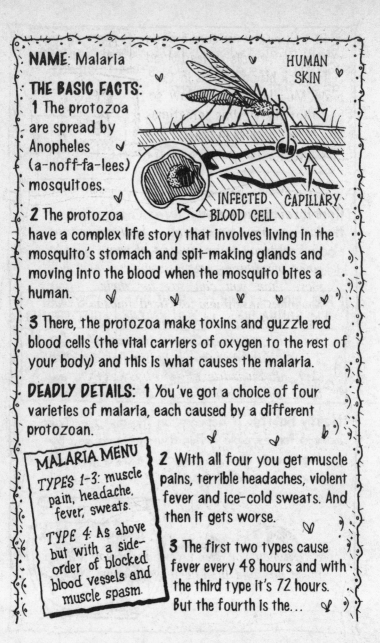

HUMAN SKIN

INFECTED BLOOD CELL   CAPILLARY

2 The protozoa have a complex life story that involves living in the mosquito's stomach and spit-making glands and moving into the blood when the mosquito bites a human.

3 There, the protozoa make toxins and guzzle red blood cells (the vital carriers of oxygen to the rest of your body) and this is what causes the malaria.

DEADLY DETAILS: 1 You've got a choice of four varieties of malaria, each caused by a different protozoan.

> **MALARIA MENU**
>
> TYPES 1-3: muscle pain, headache, fever, sweats.
>
> TYPE 4: As above but with a side-order of blocked blood vessels and muscle spasm.

2 With all four you get muscle pains, terrible headaches, violent fever and ice-cold sweats. And then it gets worse.

3 The first two types cause fever every 48 hours and with the third type it's 72 hours. But the fourth is the...

4 REALLY nasty version. Around half the victims die as dead blood cells block blood vessels in the brain. Muscle spasms follow, so bad that the victims sometimes bite their tongues in half!

FINK I'FE GOK THE FORF HYPE!

Bet you never knew!

1 There have been germs – bacteria, viruses and protozoa – for millions of years. They're some of nature's great survivors – which is more than you can say for their victims. Scientists have found fossilized dinosaur bones that had been attacked by bacteria. I expect the dinosaur was an Ouchmybonesaresaur.

2 Every day you shed ten billion flakes of dead skin – they just drop off your body as fresh skin forms underneath. You can see a few of these bits if you turn a dirty pair of black trousers inside-out. At least two-thirds of these bits carry bacteria and viruses.

3 So when you clean your room you stir up these bits and breathe in your own skin and germs!

Could you be a doctor?

A patient has a boil on his nose. The boil is caused by bacteria and the red swelling is full of lovely golden pus.

Oh well, it could be worse – it could be a boil on the foot. Then you'd have pus in boots! Anyway, what forms this substance?

a) It's gas given out by the bacteria.
b) It's blood sucked in by the bacteria.
c) It's a mixture of dead blood cells and dead bacteria.

Answer: c) The blood cells died heroically fighting the bacteria.

Want the full story? It's in a top secret deadly-disease-fighting document. And it just so happens we've got a copy and it's in the next chapter...

YOUR BATTLING BODY

Fancy a fight? Well, your body does. Every day it's spoiling for a fight – with germs! And here, as promised, is a unique glimpse of those top-secret military battle plans...

TOP SECRET DOCUMENT

KEEP OUT OF REACH OF MICROBES!

The Human Body Defence Plan   BY MAJOR GERM-BEATER

 The body's defence mechanism, or "immune system" as we insiders call it, is based on phased defence and counter-attacks ... so stand to attention for this important briefing!

MILITARY BASES AND ROADS

The defence system is based on military roads called the lymphatic (lim-fat-tic) system, complete with army checkpoints called lymph nodes, or "glands", where white blood cells re-group to fight infection.

RED BLOOD CELLS CLOT IN A NET OF FIBRIN

SCAB (DON'T PICK IT!)

SKIN

LINES OF DEFENCE

1 Skin barrier

I'd like to see the germ who can burrow through this thick leathery wall! Trouble is, humans do insist on scraping or cutting their skin and allowing germs in.

2 The snot barrier

Known to us defence professionals as "mucus". The sticky snot of the nose or windpipe or guts bogs down attackers and contains a substance that kills some germs. Our front-line troops deployed here are the mast cells. They're under orders to release a chemical they store called histamine (his-ta-meen). This widens gaps between cells in blood vessel walls – allowing killer white blood cells (see opposite) to leave the blood and fight the invaders. Meanwhile, watery snot is released to flush out the enemy!

ARGH!

FLUSH THEM OUT!

ALL NOSE-PICKERS SHOULD BE COURT-MARTIALLED!

Some humans pick snot from their noses and eat it. This disgraceful habit allows germs caught in the mucus to enter into the guts where they can cause diarrhoea if not dissolved by acid in the stomach.

3 Bloody warfare

a) As a result of the gaps forming between cells, the blood vessels naturally get larger and more blood rushes to the area making it feel hot. That's why body parts, where there are germs, appear red and swollen.

b) Germs can die if they get too hot – so we aim to make 'em sweat by heating up the blood! White blood cells send chemical signals to the brain, which responds with chemicals that cause

the body's cells to make energy faster. This gives off extra heat. The skin turns pale as blood is retained deep within the body so it doesn't lose heat to the air. Humans call this "fever" – I call it a jolly good tactic!

All army units must counter-attack with every weapon at our disposal!

WHITE BLOOD CELL ARMY UNITS...

The T-cell army
T = top secret code for thymus (thi-mus) area where the army is recruited and trained.

This army is made up of three operational units...

THYMUS

1 The killer cells are combat personnel with orders to search out and destroy all germs. All body cells believed to be hiding germs are to be eliminated without mercy!

2 T-helper cells are highly trained intelligence and communications specialists. They identify germs and produce a chemical signal alerting the B-cell army (see opposite), and order the killer cells to move in.

3 T-suppressor officer corps'. Their job is to stop the others getting carried away and attacking in too great numbers. This could result in damage to the body as, inevitably, civilian body cells will get killed in the fighting. Yes, it's tough – but this is WAR!

THE B-CELL ARMY

B = top secret military code for bone marrow training centre where the army is recruited and trained.

BONE MARROW

1 Each B-cell is trained to identify enemy antigens. That's military jargon for any invader of the body. ("Antigen" – just saying that word makes me feel dirty!) Each B-cell is covered with chemicals like tiny keys that lock into chemicals on the outside of a particular antigen. And since we have millions of different B-cells there's every chance that for any antigen we'll have a B-cell to fit it. You can rely on the B-cell army to get to grips with the enemy.

2 Specialized B-cells are based in the lymph node bases ready to make antibodies. If an

antigen is detected, the bone marrow training centre will send millions of B-cell reinforcements with the right key to search out antigens wherever they're hiding.

THE ANTIBODY WEAPON SYSTEM

These are guided missiles used by our troops to lock on to antigens and destroy them. Each antibody is designed to cover an antigen and gum it up so it can be engulfed by the tank corps (see next page).

WHITE BLOOD CELL TANK CORPS

Our tanks – we call them macrophages (mac-ro-fay-ges) – capture the gummed up enemy bacteria by grabbing them in their mechanical arms and pulling them inside. All prisoners are to be dissolved alive! Remember – WAR IS NOT A TEA PARTY!

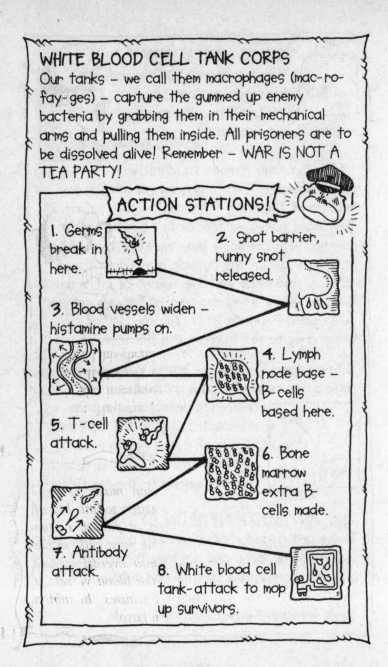

ACTION STATIONS!

1. Germs break in here.

2. Snot barrier, runny snot released.

3. Blood vessels widen – histamine pumps on.

4. Lymph node base – B-cells based here.

5. T-cell attack.

6. Bone marrow extra B-cells made.

7. Antibody attack.

8. White blood cell tank-attack to mop up survivors.

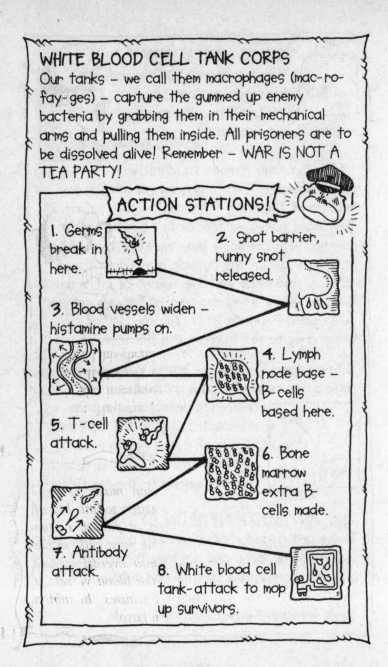

Deadly expressions

A scientist says...

Do you say...?

WELL, I THINK YOU SHOULD MIND YOUR OWN BUSINESS, BEAKY-NOSE.

Answer: He said "interferon", not *interfering*. All cells make interferon (in-ter-fear-ron) if attacked by viruses. It doesn't save them but in ways we don't understand this chemical stops the virus from multiplying.

Bet you never knew!
Your defences against disease can make you ill! Asthma sufferers are unusually sensitive to little bits of chemical like pollen from flowers or pollution from cars. When they're breathed in, the mast cells in the lungs that make histamine go into overdrive. And although this substance widens the blood vessels it actually narrows airways and causes breathing problems. It's enough to make you gasp!

183

You're probably an expert in what viruses can do to the human body. Yes, you are! If you've ever had a cold you'll know *exactly* how it feels. The bad news is that after hundreds of years of medical research even the cleverest doctors still can't cure a cold. The good news is that the body cures itself anyway. Here's how it's done...

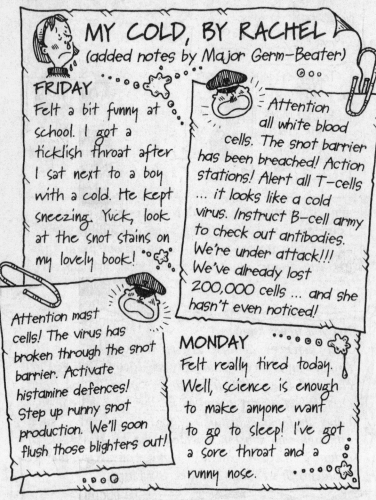

MY COLD, BY RACHEL
(added notes by Major Germ-Beater)

FRIDAY
Felt a bit funny at school. I got a ticklish throat after I sat next to a boy with a cold. He kept sneezing. Yuck, look at the snot stains on my lovely book!

Attention all white blood cells. The snot barrier has been breached! Action stations! Alert all T-cells ... it looks like a cold virus. Instruct B-cell army to check out antibodies. We're under attack!!! We've already lost 200,000 cells ... and she hasn't even noticed!

Attention mast cells! The virus has broken through the snot barrier. Activate histamine defences! Step up runny snot production. We'll soon flush those blighters out!

MONDAY
Felt really tired today. Well, science is enough to make anyone want to go to sleep! I've got a sore throat and a runny nose.

TUESDAY

I woke up today with a sore nose. It felt all bunged up. Had to go to school — worst luck. Felt chronic!

Histamine defences working well. White blood cells to the affected nose region.

WEDNESDAY

Terrible runny nose, I feel light-headed. Mum says I've got a fever. No school today.

Runny nasal discharge has germs on the run! But, oh dear – she's wiping her nose with used hankies and stuffing viruses back up her nostrils! Fever defence working well.

THURSDAY

I just feel like going to sleep. I'm so tired.

"Sleep" she says! Pah! We in the immune system NEVER sleep. We've been fighting non-stop for days. Phew!

FRIDAY

I'm tired and washed out.

Not half as much as us! We've lost millions of dead white blood cells ... but, we've won – well done chaps!!

SATURDAY

I'm feeling better! Just in time for the weekend!

All thanks to us!

Once you've had a disease caused by a virus or bacterium the general rule is that you shouldn't get it again. A scientist would say you're immune to that illness. (Yes, I know you get colds all the time but that's because each cold is caused by a slightly different virus.)

Deadly disease fact file

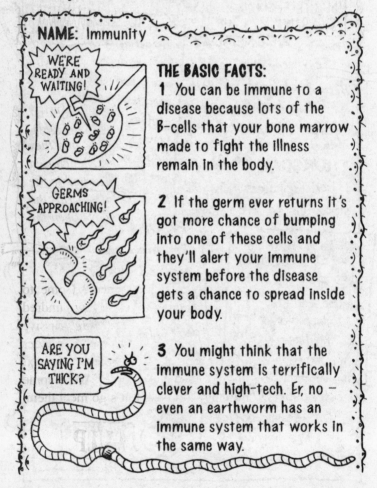

NAME: Immunity

WE'RE READY AND WAITING!

THE BASIC FACTS:

1 You can be immune to a disease because lots of the B-cells that your bone marrow made to fight the illness remain in the body.

GERMS APPROACHING!

2 If the germ ever returns it's got more chance of bumping into one of these cells and they'll alert your immune system before the disease gets a chance to spread inside your body.

ARE YOU SAYING I'M THICK?

3 You might think that the immune system is terrifically clever and high-tech. Er, no – even an earthworm has an immune system that works in the same way.

DEADLY DETAILS: If lots of people in an area are immune to a disease it can't spread widely, but if most people aren't immune then it will become a huge tidal wave of illness – an epidemic.

INFECTED PEOPLE MULTIPLY IN THE SAME WAY AS BACTERIA

COUGH!

Bet you never knew!
When an epidemic struck the cities of ancient Turkey an ugly person was chosen to be sacrificed to the gods. They ate a barley loaf, dried figs and cheese, and they were beaten with fig branches. Afterwards, the chosen person was burnt alive and their ashes scattered in the sea. Oddly enough, this practice didn't stop the epidemic and no, your teacher wouldn't have been the victim so stop daydreaming and read on...

So why aren't there epidemics everywhere? Come to think of it why aren't we all *dead*? Well, a few hundred years ago, as you'll discover later, there *were* massive outbreaks of disease but today many diseases are under control – thanks to the work of the people in the next chapter. Who are these wonderful people? Well, some people call them "miracle workers". Let's go meet them.

ANXIOUS ANTIGEN

GULP!

MEDICAL MIRACLES

In a world full of deadly diseases you can rely on two friends.

1 YOUR IMMUNE SYSTEM   **2** YOUR DOCTOR

Though if your doctor's Dr Grimgrave you'll have to make do with your immune system. Anyway, talking about medics, it's time to meet the people who dedicate their lives to fighting deadly diseases...

Spot the scientist

Let's imagine your school has been hit by a mystery ailment – the dreaded "Green Teacher Disease". Teachers and (I'm afraid) pupils, are turning green and developing smelly purple boils.

SCHOOL CLOSED DUE TO OUTBREAK OF GREEN TEACHER DISEASE!

A team of scientists is desperately trying to find a cure. Here they are. . .

① IMMUNOLOGIST

(im-mu-nol-lo-gist)
Studies how the immune
system fights the disease.
The immunologist is looking
at blood samples from the
sufferers to discover if
they're making antibodies
to fight the disease
antigens. An immunologist
knows the difference
between an antibody and an
antigen (check back to
page 181 if you're not
sure).

ABSENT-MINDED
LOOK.

TEST-TUBE
CONTAINING AN
INTERESTING
BLOOD SAMPLE.

② BACTERIOLOGIST/VIROLOGIST

Bacteriologists (back-teer-re-ol-lo-gists)
study bacteria and virologists (vi-rol-lo-
gists) study (that's right!) viruses – and
between them they are trying to find the

REMEMBER THESE?
FROM PAGES 19-24

VIRUS

BACTERIA

germs that cause Green
Teacher Disease. (They could
be bacteria or viruses – we
don't know yet.) Both
scientists want to search
for the germs in samples of
blood and skin and snot and diseased matter
from the purple boils. The bacteriologist
will try to spot the germs through a
microscope but since viruses are far
smaller than bacteria, the virologist will
use the more powerful electron microscope
for her work.

CONTINUED ▶

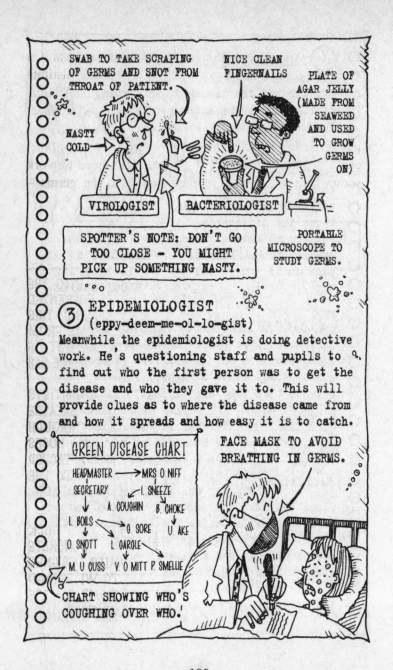

SWAB TO TAKE SCRAPING OF GERMS AND SNOT FROM THROAT OF PATIENT.

NICE CLEAN FINGERNAILS

PLATE OF AGAR JELLY (MADE FROM SEAWEED AND USED TO GROW GERMS ON)

NASTY COLD

VIROLOGIST

BACTERIOLOGIST

SPOTTER'S NOTE: DON'T GO TOO CLOSE - YOU MIGHT PICK UP SOMETHING NASTY.

PORTABLE MICROSCOPE TO STUDY GERMS.

③ EPIDEMIOLOGIST
(eppy-deem-me-ol-lo-gist)

Meanwhile the epidemiologist is doing detective work. He's questioning staff and pupils to find out who the first person was to get the disease and who they gave it to. This will provide clues as to where the disease came from and how it spreads and how easy it is to catch.

GREEN DISEASE CHART

HEADMASTER ⟶ MRS O NIFF
SECRETARY ⟶ I. SNEEZE
A. COUGHIN   B. CHOKE
L. BOILS ⟶ O. SORE   U. AKE
O. SNOTT   L. GARGLE
M. U CUSS   V. O MITT   P. SMELLIE

CHART SHOWING WHO'S COUGHING OVER WHO.

FACE MASK TO AVOID BREATHING IN GERMS.

Where they work

All these scientists work in university laboratories and in specialist research institutes such as the Pasteur Institute in Paris or the Center for Disease Control in Atlanta, USA. Immunologists also work in hospital laboratories where they advise doctors on how well patients are resisting diseases. Scientists who work with germs that cause deadly diseases are in danger. They need to work somewhere where they're protected from the germs – somewhere like this...

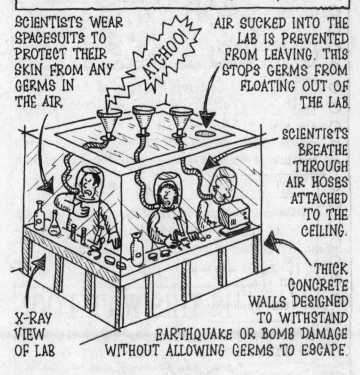

HIGH-SECURITY LAB (FOR DEADLY INCURABLE DISEASES)

SCIENTISTS WEAR SPACESUITS TO PROTECT THEIR SKIN FROM ANY GERMS IN THE AIR

ATCHOO!

AIR SUCKED INTO THE LAB IS PREVENTED FROM LEAVING. THIS STOPS GERMS FROM FLOATING OUT OF THE LAB.

SCIENTISTS BREATHE THROUGH AIR HOSES ATTACHED TO THE CEILING.

THICK CONCRETE WALLS DESIGNED TO WITHSTAND EARTHQUAKE OR BOMB DAMAGE WITHOUT ALLOWING GERMS TO ESCAPE.

X-RAY VIEW OF LAB

Could you be a scientist?

So how would you get on as a germ scientist?

1 Have you got the right gut instinct? In 1982 Australian scientist Barry Marshall became convinced that the painful ulcers some people get in their stomachs were caused by bacteria. It was a gut instinct all right – but certain germs always seemed to be in the victims' stomachs. Barry decided on an experiment...

What did he do?

a) He cut open a healthy patient's stomach and added the bacteria to see what would happen.

b) He tried growing the germs in a bowl of school dinner custard. The slimy custard was the closest he could get to the slimy insides of the stomach.

c) He drank the disgusting bacteria and stuck a viewing tube called an endoscope into his own stomach to check what they were up to.

2 In 1948 scientists were searching for a person who was spreading the germs that caused the deadly disease typhoid in their poo. How did they find the person?

a) They placed an advert in the paper.

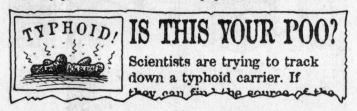

b) They tested everyone in town for the disease.

c) They ran tests on the sewage and found the germ and then tested all the sewage pipes, crawling through the sewers until they found the toilet that the person was using.

How did scientists discover that germs cause disease?

It's a good question because germs can be quite hard to investigate. They come in a confusing number of varieties and none of them carry signs saying:

Early ideas

Some ancient doctors suspected that unseen creatures caused disease. Roman medic Marcus Terentius Varro

(116-27 BC) reckoned that disease was caused by tiny living things that were too small to see. He was right, of course, but he couldn't prove it.

But despite Varro's ideas most ancient doctors thought the gods caused disease. We've brought together two of them to argue their cases...

Four hundred years ago doctors thought that diseases were caused by revolting smells. Luckily this isn't true, otherwise your brother or sister's trainers could spark a major health alert.

Even after the microscope was invented in 1609, scientists refused to believe that tiny germs could kill a person – it was like saying ants could slay elephants.

The first clue that germs were less innocent than they seemed came in the 1860s when French scientist Louis Pasteur (1822-1895) investigated a disease that attacked silkworms (the caterpillars that spin silk). Pasteur found the disease was caused by protozoa and that a nasty bacterium caused silkworm diarrhoea. But it was hard to collar a particular germ and say "Oi, you're nicked for causing this 'ere illness." For one thing, there are loads of germs which made pinning the blame on one of them a bit hit or miss.

But a pushy doctor was to change all that...

Hall of fame: Robert Koch (1843-1910)
Nationality: German

Young Robert Koch had 13 brothers and sisters. Can you imagine how he suffered? Thirteen brothers and sisters all trying to boss you around.

Well, anyway, Robert was a clever lad and his science-minded granddad and uncle encouraged him to build up a collection of dead insects and other grisly specimens. Later, at the University of Gottingen, one of his teachers persuaded young Robert to take up medicine and he became a doctor, first in the Army and later on in Wollstein, Germany.

But he became more and more interested in germs. He turned his consulting room into a lab and in 1871, his wife gave him a microscope for his birthday.

Guess what he wanted it for? No, not for searching the cat's fur for fleas. He used it to take an even closer look at germs.

And so Koch came to study an especially disgusting disease called anthrax. This causes revolting sores on the lungs and can kill humans and animals.

Koch used dyes to stain some bacteria so he could see them clearly under the microscope. He next proved that it really was these bacteria that caused the diseases by injecting them into some cute little mice and making them ill. (I suppose they could have been saved by mouse to mouse resuscitation.)

Could you be a scientist?

What did Koch feed his anthrax bacteria on?

a) Chocolate

b) Wood shavings

c) The watery jelly-like stuff from the inside of an eyeball mixed up with blood.

CLUE: Think of where anthrax bacteria might like to eat.

Answer: c) At this point agar jelly hadn't been invented. The anthrax germs happily multiplied on the tasty gloop. (Of course, anthrax is a disease of animals so the germs fed on bits of animal.) By the way, Koch invented agar jelly a few years later.

Koch had proved for the first time ever that germs cause disease in humans. And he used his work to develop four postulates.

Deadly expressions

Do you say...?

Koch's suggestions were important because they outlined a new approach to studying disease. Here's Robert Koch back from the dead to explain them.

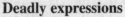

Oh – a quick warning. As a result of his discoveries he did become rather big-headed...

198

Dead brainy: the great Robert Koch

I, the great Robert Koch, will explain my four postulates that have changed the history of the world. I will use as my example the severe sore throat that I have developed since I've been dead. I've been dying for a cough in my coffin.

In order to prove that a germ causes disease...

Postulate 1. You must find the germ living in the body in the same place as the disease. I took a swab of my throat and discovered this bacterium.

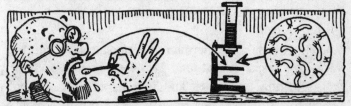

Postulate 2. You must be able to grow the germ so that it divides several times. I have succeeded in growing the germ in a plate of beef soup that has been cooked into a jelly.

Postulate 3. By giving the germs to a healthy animal you make the animal sick. I have succeeded in doing this to a rabbit.

Postulate 4. You must next find the germs living inside the animal. I have taken a sample from the rabbit and found the germs have multiplied in its throat.

THIS EXPERIMENT IS A PAIN IN THE NECK – I MEAN THROAT!

This proves that although I have been dead for some time I am still a great world-famous scientist.

Koch was right. The German government gave him his very own research institute. He also got to travel the world cutting up bodies and investigating deadly but fascinating diseases. For Koch it was a dream job. His two greatest discoveries, in 1882 and 1884, were the germs that cause the deadly diseases TB and cholera. (You can find out more on pages 165 and 240.) In 1905 Koch was awarded the Nobel Prize for his work.

POSTULATE 5 – I THOROUGHLY DESERVE IT!

BOAST!

Between them, Koch and his rival, Frenchman Louis Pasteur, encouraged a whole new group of scientists to plunge into the world of deadly diseases and go searching for the germs that caused them. And the scientists had a powerful new weapon to fight infection: vaccines. Here's all the vital facts you need to know about those necessary jabs...

Pass your science test with Horrible Science

1 What is a vaccine?

It's a sample of weakened germs. The germs can be weakened by keeping them low on food or heating them to a temperature that they find uncomfortable. Either way, the germs should find it hard to multiply – yes, a bit like some kids in a maths test, ha ha.

2 How does a vaccine work?

By injecting the germs into a person you can get their immune system (B-cells and T-cells) to recognize the germ and get ready for a bit of fisticuffs. Of course the weakened germs aren't a threat, but if the same germs get into the body the white blood cells will be ready and waiting.

ARGH! THEY'RE WAITING FOR US!

3 How were vaccines discovered?

In 1796 Edward Jenner (1749-1823) discovered how to use pus from the sores made by the milder disease, cowpox, to prevent smallpox. Although Jenner didn't understand about immunity, the virus that causes cowpox is similar to smallpox so the body can use immunity against one to fight the other. Jenner was on the right lines even if his scratch wasn't a true vaccine because he didn't use actual smallpox germs. Then, in 1879 Louis Pasteur investigated chicken cholera. (Any guesses what animal this disease infects?)

Pasteur went on holiday leaving a sample of the germs in a nice tasty broth – lucky no one ate it whilst he was away. On his return, Pasteur was amazed to find that when he injected the disease into, yes, you got it, chickens – the birds *didn't* fall ill. As Pasteur found out, the weakened germs made the chickens immune to the disease. Bet that gave him something to crow about!

New drug facts

The doctors soon had another weapon. Scientists were rapidly discovering that certain substances killed bacteria but not the living cells of the body that they lived amongst...

1 The first germ-killing substance was salvarsan, found by German scientist Paul Ehrlich (1854-1915) in 1909. Ehrlich had been searching for new germ-killing substances and salvarsan was effort number 606. And I thought third time was supposed be lucky, not 606th!

2 Many early germ-killing drugs were actually dyes. German scientists noticed that the dyes stained and killed bacteria and left human cells untouched. One famous example was prontosil found by Gerhard Domagk in 1932 (1895-1964). Unfortunately the red dye turned the patient bright red!

3 Within four years French scientists had found that the germ-killing part of the drug was actually a substance called sulphonamide (sul-fon-a-myde) that had already been discovered in 1908. So poor Domagk was left red in the face.

4 Scientists began to develop new drugs based on the sulphonamide chemicals and by 1947 they had made over 5,000 varieties!

Oddly enough though, some of the most powerful germ-killing substances are made not in test tubes but in living cells. Wonderful chemicals that rescue people from the jaws of death. Why not inject a bit of life into your day and read the next chapter?

It could prove a lifesaver...

LUCKY LIFESAVERS

Doctors have two more weapons in the battle against deadly disease: antitoxins and antibiotics. And if you thought I said "ant-tick-tock" (an insect alarm clock?) you'd better read this next bit...

Amazing antitoxins

Antitoxins are antibodies from a person or animal that has had a disease. They can be injected into another person to help them fight the disease, a process also known as "serum therapy". This breakthrough was made by two scientists working for Robert Koch, German Emil von Behring (1854-1917) and Japanese Shibasaburo Kitasato (1852-1931).

Could you be a scientist?

The scientists injected toxins from a deadly kind of bacteria called tetanus into a rabbit. The rabbit hadn't received enough toxin to kill it and it made antibodies to the toxins. The scientists then injected these into mice. They then gave the toxins to the mice.

What happened?

a) The mice grew extra long ears and nibbled lettuce.

b) The mice stayed healthy.

c) The mice died.

Answer: b) The rabbit antitoxins protected the mice. In 1894 Von Behring used this technique to get a horse to make antitoxins that could be given to children to fight the deadly disease diphtheria.

A note to the reader...

Homework can be a problem – especially when you haven't done it. Nowadays, teachers are quite sophisticated and no longer believe perfectly reasonable excuses like:

What you need is a new set of excuses – like you're suffering from a deadly disease. If you're lucky you might even get the next six weeks off school! Anyway, free with this book you get a set of sick notes. Simply copy them out and fill in your name in the spaces and post them to your teacher!

Sickening sick note 1: Diphtheria

Dear teacher,
I'm really scared about poor little ~~me~~
.... ~~I've~~ s/he's got
disgusting, oozing throat sores and now
they've formed a horrible thick slimy
layer. It's TERRIBLE! Poor ....
can't drink soup without it dribbling
out of her/his nostrils! Her/his
condition is dreadfully desperate - s/he
can hardly breathe! The doctor says
it's diphtheria - so I hope you'll
understand that .... hasn't done
any ~~of my~~ homework.
Signed,

A concerned parent

Sickening sick note notes

1 With diphtheria, the bacteria make toxins that poison the nerves and stop them from working. This can lead to heart failure and death.

2 And if that doesn't happen the victim is slowly suffocated by the slimy germs. No wonder the Spanish call the disease "garrotillo" from "garrotte" – a form of strangulation.

CHOKE A LOT?

I'M SUFFOCATING AND YOU'RE OFFERING ME SWEETS?

3 But on the plus side you do get a few days off school ... and maybe more!

The bravest dog in the world

Nome, Alaska, January 1925

Anna was dying. The nine-year-old girl had little time left but mercifully she didn't know it. Her breathing was uneasy as the diphtheria took a grip. Outside, the wind howled and snow banked up above the windows. It seemed that Nome Hospital was lost in a vast, icy wilderness.

Dr Ferguson paced up and down the ward. He was thin and haggard and his eyes hadn't closed for two nights. Five times the town's radio operator had called for help for the sick children in his care. All had diphtheria and they needed antitoxin desperately.

But when would help come?

Already five children were dead, slowly smothered by the germs that bred in their throats. Twenty-five children were sick, of whom Anna was the worst. And Ferguson knew that without antitoxin the disease would kill them all, one by one.

He glared angrily at the swirling snow. If only the weather would ease, a supply might get through! But it kept on snowing – for hour after hour until the drifts were higher than a house.

Next morning, Americans read in their newspapers of the plight of the children. In churches all over the country prayers were offered but everyone knew that prayers wouldn't be enough. Only antitoxin could save the children and a supply was sent to the railhead town of Nenana – but this was over 500 miles from Nome. In this weather all the planes were grounded and an appeal went out to dog sledge drivers.

"I've heard about the kids," growled driver George Kasson, "and I wanna help."

"Great – when can you go?" asked the stressed-out hospital chief at Nenana.

George held up a big work-roughened hand. "That's the good news. The bad news is that it's gonna take nine days to get to Nome."

"*Nine days!*" the official gasped. "The kids don't have that kinda time! For pity's sake, George, you're a top driver! You've got to get there faster!"

Kasson shook his head firmly. "It's 500 miles of white hell. Nine days is the record, and in this weather it could take 20."

The hospital chief swore and thumped his desk.

***

Dr Ferguson heard of the delay but dared not tell his nurses. One of them was Anna's mother. She could see that her daughter was desperately sick and every so often she would creep into the kitchen and sob quietly. Yes, Anna was still alive and fighting every step of the way. But now her body was tired, desperately weak, and her throat was partly blocked by a veil of germs so that she could no longer swallow. Ferguson knew that she couldn't hold out much longer.

And outside it was still snowing...

Three days and 300 miles later, George Kasson braced himself to control the heavy sledge as it hissed through the endless snow and biting wind.

The snow had frozen to his beard and he had to keep wiping his snow goggles and screw up his eyes against the glare of the whiteness around him. With grim pride he noted that his 13 dogs were pulling well. They were all champions, especially the lead dog, Balto, the biggest and strongest of them all. But the temperature was still dropping...

Kasson shivered. He had gooseflesh even under layers of fur clothing. How cold was it? Minus forty, minus fifty, minus sixty? Even he had never known such bitter weather. The falling snow was becoming a blizzard.

At the hospital at Nome, Anna's mother watched her daughter's face by the light of an oil lamp. The child was so deathly pale she might have been a waxwork, except for a thin film of sweat. But every few seconds she would draw a painful breath, a kind of gasp. And once her eyes opened. She gazed calmly at her mother and said:

"I feel ... awful. I'm not dying, am I?"

And Anna's mother had kissed and hugged her daughter, saying, "Hush darling, don't talk. I'm here."

Dr Ferguson touched his nurse on the shoulder. She turned and said: "I just thought it was a sore throat, something that would clear up. It's my fault – it's all my fault!"

"Get some sleep," he said wearily. "There's nothing we can do tonight."

Kasson could see only a white blur. Slowly he sensed that the glare from the snow had almost blinded him. Sightless, he could no longer guide the dogs but in any case there was no light, no landmark, nothing to show the way. Kasson could feel that the dogs were tiring now, although Balto was pulling as hard as ten dogs. It was almost as if the animal sensed the urgency of the mission.

But where were they? Where were they heading?

Kasson heard only the howl of the wind against his fur hood and the endless hiss of the sledge runners and the occasional barks of the exhausted dogs.

His mind slid in and out of consciousness.

Dawn was a lightness around the white blur of Kasson's damaged vision. He removed his goggles and tried to look around. A little distance away he could just make out buildings half-buried by snow.

Where was he? Nome? No, impossible. Yes – yes, YES! They had reached Nome! A shout echoed off the hills. A disbelieving shout and then another shout, "He's here! HE'S HERE!" Excited locals on skis joined the sledge.

A crowd gathered in the main street shouting and cheering, dancing for joy in the cold morning air. People were hugging Kasson and petting the dogs, especially Balto, who stood silent with exhaustion, too weary now to wag his tail.

The shouts reached the hospital and all the nurses were hugging each other with delight and joining an ecstatic Dr Ferguson as he unloaded the precious antitoxin. All the nurses were there, except one who stood by Anna's bedside with tears streaming down her face.

"You're safe now," she whispered to the unconscious girl. "You're going to live."

Bet you never knew!

It was a miracle. Despite his temporary blindness, George Kasson had reached Nome in an incredible five days, and thanks to his bravery all the children were saved. Today in Central Park in New York children play on a statue of Balto. It was unveiled at a special ceremony at which George and his dog were guests of honour. Balto got over-excited after sniffing a lady dog in the crowd – but no one minded because he was THE BRAVEST DOG IN THE WORLD!

Amazing antibiotics

Three years later a scientist discovered an amazing substance called an antibiotic that killed bacteria (but not viruses). The substance was made into a new drug called penicillin that could literally snatch people from the jaws of death, and its discoverer won the Nobel Prize and became an international superstar. His name was Alexander Fleming (1881-1955) and he's so famous your teacher will know all about him – won't she/he?

Well, *won't* she/he? Let's find out...

OF COURSE I KNOW ALL ABOUT ALEXANDER FLIM, ER, FLOM, ER, FLAM, ER...

FLEMING!

Test your teacher

1 How did Fleming get his first medical job?

a) His natural genius impressed other scientists.

b) He was a crack rifle shot.

c) The other scientists needed someone to make tea.

2 During the First World War Fleming treated wounded soldiers in France. What experiment did he perform to help them?

a) He used slug juice to heal wounds.

b) He made a model wound and filled it with germs to test whether germ-killing chemicals worked properly.

c) He tried to use cold tea to kill germs.

3 What was Fleming's favourite hobby?

a) Gardening.

b) Painting pictures using germs.

c) Collecting used tea bags.

4 In 1921 Fleming discovered the germ-killing chemical in mucus. How did he make this breakthrough?

a) A dollop of snot fell from his nose on to a sample of germs.

b) He made the substance by mixing chemicals in a test tube.

c) He found that tea leaves didn't rot when they were wrapped in a snotty handkerchief.

Answers: 1 b) No, Fleming DIDN'T shoot his boss at the job interview! The hospital where Fleming was a student had a prize-winning rifle team. Fleming was a member of the team and his bosses were keen for him to stay.

2 b) Fleming melted some glass into the shape of a revolting deep jagged wound. He found that germs could lurk in the corners of the wound where germ-killing chemicals couldn't reach them. This encouraged Fleming to treat wounds by washing them and bandaging them rather than using the chemicals.

3 b) Fleming painted pictures using germs. Different germs have different colours and Fleming drew the pictures in agar jelly with needles dipped in the germs. The germs grew on the jelly to form the picture. Fancy one on your wall?

4 a) One day Fleming had a cold and snot from his runny nose fell on some germs and killed them.

(Unfortunately the germ-killing chemical, lysozyme, wasn't powerful enough to make into a drug but Fleming became interested in natural germ-killers.)

What your teacher's score means
0-1 Lucky the school inspectors didn't hear about this.

2-3 Fair, but remind your teacher that a higher score will be required the next time you test them.
4 Too good to be true.
Note all the **c)** answers seem to be about tea and if your teacher kept saying "**c**)" it's probably because she's longing for a tea-break. This attitude is not acceptable in one who is supposed to be educating the young.

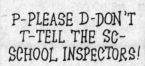

P-PLEASE D-DON'T T-TELL THE SC- SCHOOL INSPECTORS!

A mouldy old story

It's a fact that raw penicillin is made by a rare type of mould that Fleming found growing on one of his agar plates. The story has often been told but here's a *Horrible Science* exclusive – the mould gets to tell its *own* story!

MY STORY
BY PENNY CILLIUM

Surprised you want to talk to *me*. Me being an 'umble mould and all that. In all these years no one's ever asked for *my* side of the story, even though it was me and me mouldy friends what made this stuff millions of years before humans got their hands on it. Well, anyway 'ere's what *really* happened.

I first saw the light of day in St. Mary's hospital, back in 1928. A scientist was researching moulds and I started my life as a little spore what blew upstairs and landed on a plate of jelly in Fleming's lab. *Strawberry or lime?* I asked meself. Sorry, just a mouldy joke. The jelly was boiled seaweed. But I'm not fussy – if it's food, it's food.

Fleming was growing bacteria from an infected boil on the plate – but I soon put a stop to that. Well, I mean, I know I'm only 'umble but would you want someone oozing boils over your dinner? So I squirted some germ-killing stuff we moulds make and that kept the germs away. Success on a plate, I thought.

GRRR!

So where was Fleming whilst I was hard at

216

work? Well, I'm only an 'umble mould and no one tells me nothing but I found out later he was on holiday. Scotland to be exact – very nice! And get this ... when he comes back he only dumps me in a bucket of disinfectant! Lucky, I was on top of the pile of other plates otherwise no one would have heard of penicillin!

Wasn't till a pal of his dropped by and spotted me that Fleming got interested. That's when the trouble started – he started doing tests and one of his mates nibbled me to see if I was poisonous! Wish I had been!!! In the end Fleming used me juice to kill unwanted germs on his precious germ dishes. And that was me life for years – cleaning up for a lazy scientist! I'm only 'umble, but well, would you want to spend yer life washing dishes?

Years later humans learnt how to make my juice stronger using chemicals and people started saying what a hero lazy old Fleming was for finding me! Fleming and his mates got a Nobel Prize and a slap-up dinner – but did I get invited? I'm only 'umble – I'd have been happy to eat the mouldy old food scraps no one wanted! After all, that's a feast for me! But I was left stuck on that jelly dish and then can yer believe it? – I got shoved in a *museum*. Well honestly – there's gratitude for yer!

So what happened next?

After Fleming spotted the mould and realized it could kill germs he got excited. The problem, as we've seen, was that Fleming's mould juice wasn't strong enough to kill germs in the body. Fleming tried investigating bits of mouldy old cheese and old books and creaky old boots and household dirt, looking for more moulds with germ-killing powers. But he never found any.

PASS ME THAT CHEESY OLD SOCK, PLEASE.

WANTED! ANYTHING MOULDY. THE MOULDIER THE BETTER!

Penicillin only saw the light of day because German-born scientist Ernst Chain (1906-1979) was looking for a germ-killing substance and read an article Fleming had written about his discovery. Chain found a way to concentrate the mould juice and make it more powerful by treating it with chemicals. Now the mould juice could really prove its worth. A little girl at St. Mary's Hospital was dying from a diseased bone marrow but huge doses of penicillin cured her in just one amazing night. By morning she was sitting up in bed feeling much better!

YESTERDAY I WAS DYING AND TODAY I'M DYING... TO GO HOME!

Chain and his Australian boss Howard Florey (1898-1968) took their idea to America, looking for help to produce penicillin on a massive scale. They found backers in a government lab in Peoria, Illinois, where scientists grew the mould on waste from corn-processing. Then local fungi expert "Mouldy" Mary Hunt found another mould growing on a melon in a local market.

It turned out that this mould, a relative of the one that Fleming had found, was even better at making germ-killing juice! And for ten years, until scientists learnt how to make the drug in a test tube, this mould supplied the world with penicillin.

Amazing mould facts

1 Yep – there's no doubt about it, moulds are good for you. Well, some are. In the Ukraine and parts of England mouldy slices of bread were used as traditional bandages. And yes, the mould stopped germs from infecting the wounds.

2 You might never have been treated with penicillin but if you've ever eaten Stilton cheese you've *eaten* it. That's because a mould related to the one that makes the drug gives stilton its delicious pongy flavour.

3 Scientists have since found more mouldy antibiotics. One type are the cephalosporins (cef-fal-lo-spoor-rins) made by a kind of fungus. They were found by Italian scientist Giuseppe Brotzu by a seaside sewage pipe. The fungi were greedily scoffing the rotting poo. But NO, paddling in sewage doesn't always guarantee a great scientific discovery so don't try it.

4 Another antibiotic was discovered by American scientist Selman Waksman (1888-1973). Glory-hunting Selman was so keen he tested over 10,000 (yes, you did read that right, TEN THOUSAND) suitable fungi. Phew!

5 He found what he was looking for in the throat of a sick hen!

Waksman discovered the sickened chicken had a fungus growing in its throat. A fungus that killed other germs even whilst it was making the fowl feel foul. The scientist discovered more fungus by grovelling in the hen coop amongst the smelly droppings – but it *was* worth it, because in 1952 he won the Nobel Prize.

Deadly expressions

A scientist says...

IT'S STREPTOMYCES
(STREP-TOE-MY-SEES)

Do you say...?

IT'S STEPPED IN YOUR WHAT?

Answer: No. It's the name of the fungus Waksman found.

Streptomyces proved good for bumping off the bacteria that cause plague. These horrific germs make the other microbes you've seen so far seem warm and caring!

Wanna know more? I hope so cos THEY'RE LURKING IN THE NEXT CHAPTER

RAGING PLAGUE

This is a story about a human, a rat, a flea and a bacterium. It tells how the bacterium made everyone's lives (and deaths) a complete misery and how between them they killed hundreds of millions of people and caused hundreds of years of misery. Would you fancy a dose of plague? Why not read on – it's the most painless way to find out!

Sickening sick notes 2: the plague (aka the BLACK DEATH)

Dear teacher,
TERRIBLE NEWS! My poor little
.... had the Black Death last
night so s/he didn't do ~~my~~ any
homework. It all began with an
agonizing headache and fever and then
~~my~~ her/his lymph nodes filled with
germs and pus and swelled to the size
of apples! S/he was in AGONY!
Horrible lumps of bacteria formed under
her/his skin causing black blotches – I
don't know what to do! He/she might
die and then ~~I~~ he/she might not go to
school for ages!
Signed,
~~Me~~ A con very concerned parent.

Sickening sick note notes

(Don't forget to read this bit!)

1 Plague is caused by a bacterium called *Yersina pestis*. But this tiny pest is far from tiny in its effects. If the disease isn't treated with antibiotics at least one third of its victims *die* in five days.

2 Sometimes plague attacks the brain and blood and sometimes it dissolves the lungs. The victims cough germs everywhere and spread the disease.

3 Whatever happens, death is usually caused by the toxins that the germs make and huge lumps of germs breaking up vital bits of the body.

Sounds like fun, I DON'T think. But how does this horrible disease spread? Well, let's imagine a rat, a flea, a human and the bacterium all kept diaries... (OK – this *is* going to take quite a leap of imagination, or in the flea's case quite a hop.)

Deadly diaries

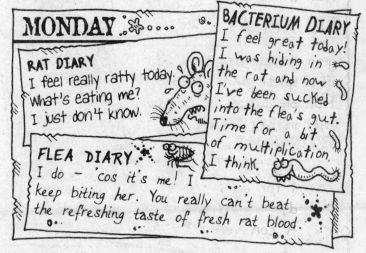

223

FLEA DIARY
I feel sick – I can't keep nothing down. Every time I suck blood I end up sicking it up! Silly me – must have drunk some dodgy blood – I'm hopping mad with myself!

BACTERIUM DIARY
Too right, pal, and now there's thousands of us blocking your gut so you can't eat properly. Well, all I can say is ... that flea's got guts!

FLEA DIARY
Still feeling peckish though. So I'm biting everything in sight trying to find some blood I can keep down.

BACTERIUM DIARY
Ha ha, every time he does that we get into another body.

THURSDAY

HUMAN DIARY · Ouch, wretched fleas! Hop it!

THE FOLLOWING WEDNESDAY...

BACTERIUM DIARY
OK gang let's move into our human victim.

HUMAN DIARY
I feel terrible. I've got fever, I'm throwing up all the time, I've got huge lumps under my arms. Er, gotta dash!

224

BACTERIUM DIARY
So you should – you've got 100,000,000 (one hundred million) of us in every drop of your blood. Hey gang – let's go and check out the old lungs.

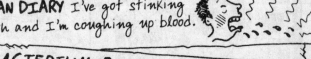

FRIDAY

HUMAN DIARY I've got stinking breath and I'm coughing up blood.

BACTERIUM DIARY
Hmm, don't reckon this one will last much longer. It's about time we found another victim ... anyone fancy a nice juicy rat?

Bet you never knew!
1 Rats actually find the plague more deadly than humans but who cares about them? Actually, I've heard some teachers have pet rats and cuddle these vicious rodents and call them soppy names like Tufty – but it's hard to imagine.
2 Although the main way the flea passes on the bacteria to humans is through bites, other methods include...
a) Rubbing flea poo into the open wound made by the bite. (Flea poo always contains bacteria.)
b) Crunching a flea in your mouth. The flea blood is full of bacteria and if it gets on your tonsils the bacteria can sometimes ooze into your blood. Lovely!

225

So that's how the bacteria can get into your body. But where did the plague come from? Who got it first – the rats, the fleas or the humans? Well, the loathsome life story of the plague is about to be revealed...

Your early life was rather obscure wasn't it? It's thought that you lived in Central Asia.

Well, yes it was over 100,000 years ago but my memory's a bit hazy now. I do remember being happy living amongst the wild marmots in their warm burrows.

They never got a nasty disease?

No, I got on well with them. Well, all right, their immune systems stopped me multiplying but they couldn't wipe me out.

Then you teamed up with your long-suffering partners the black rat and its fleas. Together you travelled the world living in ships and houses.

Er yes, but we've never got on very well.

And here they are...

Grrr – you make us sick – we're going to get you!

Er hi guys!

Yeah – it was a busy time.

You soon got to know millions of people all over Asia and Europe. When you arrived in Constantinople in AD 542, 10,000 were dying every day.

227

You made many return trips to Europe and Asia, in 1348 for instance, when over 50 million people died.

Oh yes — happy days!

The death toll was so terrible that the war then raging between England and France had to be put on hold.

Just doing my bit for world peace.

And of course you kept coming back every few years.

Well, yes, my public needed me!

But they hated you, they feared you — YOU KILLED THEM!

Yeah, OK — so I did. Now clear off BEFORE I KILL YOU!

The putrid plague

Every few years the plague struck cities all over Europe killing old and young, rich and poor. And wherever the plague went it spread sorrow, misery and death. Often people fled their homes to get away from the disease and families split up.

IT'S THE PLAGUE. FLEE!

DO THEY MEAN ME?

Of course the authorities did all they could do to fight the menace (which wasn't a lot). Which of these anti-plague rules are genuine?

Plague rules OK?

Answer TRUE or FALSE.

To fight ye plague...

1 All ye cats and dogs must be killed (and that goes for ye – Tiddles).

2 Everyone coming from plague-stricken areas must spend up to 40 days in isolation from the rest of ye town.

3 Everyone who hath the plague is to be made to take a nice hot bath twice a day on pain of ye death.

4 Paint a red cross on ye door and order ye entire family to stay at home. Leave food and medicine on ye doorstep and send ye old women to check if they be dead yet.

5 If anyone sneaks out they will be executed in front of their own house.

6 Anyone with ye plague is to be given £100 on condition that they leave town at once.

7 If ye fall sick of ye plague ye house will be burnt down and all ye belongings burnt.

Answers: 1 True. In London in 1665 plague killed 75,000 people and all the cats and dogs were killed to stop the plague spreading. In fact, cats and dogs do actually suffer from the disease but killing them did little good because, of course, the fleas carried on biting humans and spreading the disease.

2 True. This precaution was developed in Ragusa (now in Croatia) in 1377. It became known as quarantine and when it was properly enforced it stopped the plague from spreading.

3 False. In 1348 doctors at the University of Paris warned that bathing opened up pores in the skin and would let diseases into the body. This was "pore" advice. But nowadays children are still forced to take a bath on pain of death.

4 True. This is what happened in London in 1665. Unfortunately when we say "old women" we're not talking sweet white-haired old dears – we're talking killer grannies. The old women often robbed the dead and strangled those who weren't quite dead enough. In 1348 gravediggers committed this grisly crime in Florence, Italy.

5 True. This was a rule from Scotland. In 1530 a tailor was hanged in front of his house for going to church when his wife was ill. Luckily the rope broke so the man was kicked out of town instead.

6 False.

7 True. Queen Elizabeth of England (1533-1603) ordered the belongings of sick people to be burned – this was sensible because the fire killed the fleas. The same is true for burning houses, a measure used in Hawaii in 1899. Unfortunately the fire lit in one house got out of control and destroyed 5,000 more. I expect the person responsible got a warm reception.

Bet you never knew!
In the English village of Eyam in 1665 a bundle of cloth sent from the plague-stricken city of London brought fleas and the plague. Within four days the man who had received the cloth was dead. Bravely, the villagers decided to quarantine their village, letting no one in or out so that the plague wouldn't spread. Then one by one, they died. By the following spring, of the 350 villagers, just 84 were left alive. But it was thanks to their bravery that the plague spread no further.

Of course, the true causes of plague hadn't been discovered yet. But doctors tried every cure you can think of and a few that you'd never think of in a thousand years. Needless to say they were as useless as an odour-free stink bomb.

HORRIBLE HEALTH WARNING!

Did you hear me? I said they were U-S-E-L-E-S-S. So don't even *think* of trying any of these cures on yourself or your little brother/sister/pet plague rat. Some of these "cures" were DANGEROUS!

Ye Olde Plague Cure Book

Chapter One

WEAR YE RIGHT GEAR
(1348 version)

Doctors all over Europe are wearing ye latest anti-plague gear. Ye high-tech clobber will keep ye plague away!

Beak full of nice smelling herbs

Mask

Wand for checking a victim's pulse

Long leather gloves

Leather gown

SCIENTIFIC NOTE
This gear didn't stop the fleas biting the doctor and causing plague.

Chapter Two
A BREATH OF FRESH AIR

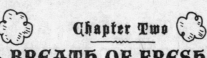

As everyone knows, ye plague be caused by some kind of nasty smell in ye air. So it helps if you...

Light ye bonfires or set off ye cannon. Smoke gets rid of ye smell. Smoking tobacco is _good_ for ye because it gets rid of smells. Everyone should smoke including ye children.

HISTORICAL NOTE: Cannons and tobacco were seventeenth century, the others were 1348. Children were beaten by their teacher at Eton College, England, for _not_ smoking.

WHACK!

BUT SMOKING IS BAD FOR YOU!

DING!

DONG!

To get ye air moving in a healthy way try letting birds fly round ye room or ringing a few bells. If ye don't have ye gunpowder or ye birds or ye bells ye needs to fart into ye bottle and uncork it to let out ye odour. Ye whiff will chase out ye foul air that causeth plague (and ye friends too). If ye have not ye bottle why not simply stick ye head down ye blocked toilet?

YE FARTY PONG!

233

BATHING IS GOOD FOR YE

No, we do not mean baths in <u>water</u> – everyone knoweth that they be <u>terribly</u> bad for ye. No, ye modern 1348 way to ward off ye plague is to bath in...

a) Vinegar

b) Your own pee (if any be left over ye can drink it twice a day)

c) Goat's pee

Chapter Four

GOOD HEALTHY SKIN: REMEDIES FROM YE SEVENTEENTH CENTURY.

If ye hath the plague ye must take care of ye skin, so...

1 Take one toad and crush it and smear ye slimy juices all over ye plague sores.

2 Rub the rump of a dead chicken on ye plague sores.

 3 Apply the guts of a PUPPY to ye forehead.

Chapter Five

MARVELLOUS MEDICINES

Now it be time for ye medicine. That'll cure ye plague in the twinkling of an eyeball! Well, maybe.

1 Eat some crunchy dry scabs from ye plague victim's sores. They be delicious washed down with a bowl of fresh pus. (Fourteenth century)

Scabs

pus

2 Fancy something with a bit more bite? Here be a traditional seventeenth-century recipe...

a) Take the brains of a young man that hath died violently.

b) Mash well and add some wine.

c) Add a generous dollop of ye horse dung and leave to rot for a year.

NOT TO BE TAKEN BEFORE 1666

That'll doeth ye trick!

Science closes in on the plague germs

In 1855 plague was on the move again. It hit the Chinese province of Yunnan and over the next 40 years killed 100,000 people. When at last it reached the coast of China it attacked ports such as Hong Kong, and ships took the rats, the fleas, the bacteria and the plague all over the world.

Between 1896 and 1917, in India alone, over *ten million* people died. Something had to be done!

By now scientists understood that germs cause disease and thanks to Koch they knew how to perform tests to discover which germ caused a particular disease. Or so they reckoned...

In 1894 a team of scientists from Robert Koch's Institute went to Hong Kong to find the plague germ. They were led by renowned scientist Shibasaburo Kitasato (remember him from page 204). But there was another scientist in the field, Swiss-born Alexandre Yersin (1863-1943) who had worked for Louis Pasteur and had since been travelling and making maps in Vietnam. But who would make the key breakthrough?

Here's how Yersin might have recorded the next few days...

YERSIN'S DIARY 1894

SATURDAY ~ Got to Hong Kong today. Phew, it's hot – had to carry all my own bags to the humble boarding house where I'm staying. Kitasato and his 30 assistants have taken over a posh hotel in the centre of town. Well, he's welcome to it. Huh, who needs a posh place ... haven't got any nice clothes to wear anyway.

MONDAY ~ Went to the local hospital today looking for a plague victim to study and got kicked out! Seems everyone reckons that Kitasato is going to find the germ. Then the man himself turns up in his smart white suit and looks at me as if I'm something the cat brought in. OK, my armpits were a bit sweaty and I guess I could have done with a shave this morning. "You're too late, Yersin!" he sneers with a smug smile. "I've already found the germ. It was simple, I grew it from the finger of a dead plague victim!"

WEDNESDAY ~ Everyone thinks Kitasato has found the germ – but I'm not so sure. I mean, whoever heard of anyone getting plague in their finger? Lungs maybe, or lymph nodes but a finger? Anyway there's a gang of English sailors burying the dead bodies and I'm bribing them to let me cut out the rotting swollen lymph nodes from the bodies. It's smelly work, but hey ... I'm a scientist, I'm used to it. S'cuse me while I throw up!

FRIDAY ~ I've found it!!! The lymph nodes are full of fat little germs! Now all I have to do is grow them. But am I on the right track or am I wasting my time? Maybe Kitasato was right after all!

SATURDAY ~ Today I injected my germs into a healthy rat. Lucky my landlord, Yu Pai-now, doesn't know there's a rat in my room. Now all I can do is wait. Will the rat get the plague?

WEDNESDAY ~ The rat's still healthy ... oh rats! Not even a sniffle!

THURSDAY ~ No, wait, the rat's got swollen glands. He's acting as if he's drunk – he's got the plague! He's very ill. Oh yes, yes, YES – I'm so very happy!

Yersin had found the germ that causes plague and that's how it came to be named *Yersina pestis*, in his honour. Back in France he was able to make an antitoxin to the germ's toxins and two years later he was back in Hong Kong to try it out. For the first time in history people were actually cured of the plague! Today, although the plague is still around – wild animals in Asia and parts of the United States carry the disease – it can be beaten by drugs and antibiotics. The plague is still feared but it's no longer a mass killer.

Mind you, if the plague seems a pain in the guts wait till you read the next chapter...

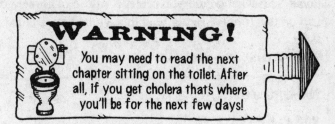

WARNING!

You may need to read the next chapter sitting on the toilet. After all, if you get cholera that's where you'll be for the next few days!

CRUEL CHOLERA

Fancy a bite to eat? Well, you'd better enjoy it now because as you read this chapter you may find your appetite disappearing. And it'll be all down to the vicious little bug that causes cholera.

What's in a name?
Here's a Greek word that your teacher doesn't know: "kholera" means diarrhoea in Greek. So next time you have a bad case of the trots tell your teacher you've got a dose of cholera and you might get six months off school! But calling cholera "diarrhoea" is like calling the *Titanic* a "boat". So what would you prefer – a dose of cholera or a trip on the *Titanic*? Better read this whilst you decide...

Deadly disease fact file

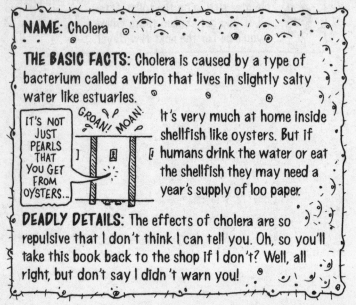

NAME: Cholera

THE BASIC FACTS: Cholera is caused by a type of bacterium called a vibrio that lives in slightly salty water like estuaries.

IT'S NOT JUST PEARLS THAT YOU GET FROM OYSTERS...

It's very much at home inside shellfish like oysters. But if humans drink the water or eat the shellfish they may need a year's supply of loo paper.

DEADLY DETAILS: The effects of cholera are so repulsive that I don't think I can tell you. Oh, so you'll take this book back to the shop if I don't? Well, all right, but don't say I didn't warn you!

A disgusting diary

Here's the journal of a Victorian lady recording the illness of her husband. Our old chum Dr Grimgrave has added his up-to-date medical comments...

Monday 1832

Oh alas! My poor Johnnie is sick. He has vomited many times and has (dare I mention this unseemly word even in the privacy of my own diary?) diarrhoea. Yet he has eaten nothing today, and prior to falling ill he had drunk but a little water. Oh woe is me! Oh woe is Johnnie!

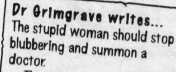

Dr Grimgrave writes...
The stupid woman should stop blubbering and summon a doctor.

The water was crawling with cholera germs. Their toxins stop the patients bowels from doing their job of soaking up digestive juices. All these juices, containing water and minerals vital to health, are flowing out of him as diarrhoea. Without prompt treatment the patient will end up a "stiff" as we say in the medical profession.

Tuesday

Alas, poor Johnnie is worse! He is feverish and his bowels are in a constant flux and producing those unmentionable fluids. He is thirsty but sicks up anything he drinks and — horrors! —: his skin has turned BLUE! And he is in agony from cramps. I called the doctor and he said he had to take blood from my beloved because he has too much! But alas — my Johnnie's blood has turned into black syrup!

Wednesday

Alas, my Johnnie is up with the angels. His skin had turned purple, then dark blue and black. And his poor dead face resembles a skull. But wait — even as I write he moves... ARGGGH! His dead body is jerking and twitching!

Dr Grimgrave writes...
That doctor should be struck off! The patient is drying out — he needs *more* liquid — not *less* blood! The drying out causes the cramps and black blood — which in turn explains the blue skin. The diarrhoea contains tiny bits of guts — hmm — I think this calls for closer examination.

Dr Grimgrave writes...
Well, the patient died as I predicted. The lack of vital body salts is resulting in signals from the dead nerves which in turn keep the dead muscles moving for a few hours. Hmm – it's a dead fascinating post-mortem phenomenon.

Sounds horrible? Sounds so horrible that you'd run a mile to get away from this disease? Well, if you don't feel like running a mile you could always take a nice relaxing holiday in some of the cholera hot-spots.

HORRIBLE SCIENCE HOLIDAYS present
A HOLIDAY WITH A DIFFERENCE
THE CHOLERA EXPERIENCE

Visit some of the most spectacular and beautiful parts of the world and spend hours and hours on the toilet (don't forget to pack the loo paper!). You'll be dying to get away!

Paris 1832
Enjoy the colour of the Paris carnival. Marvel at the revellers with their delightful painted faces and bright costumes.

CONTINUED ➤

243

SMALL PRINT

1. The revellers with blue faces are actually suffering from cholera but everyone thought it was just make-up until they started dying in the streets.

2 If you're not French it might be a good idea to make yourself scarce. The crowd blamed foreigners for poisoning the victims and started killing them!

3. For the REAL cholera experience why not try one of the cures suggested by Dr Francois Megendie. You lie down and he slaps 50 slimy blood-sucking leeches on your body. Note – it doesn't work, but hey, it's an experience!

FANCY A BIT OF ADVENTURE?

Try a trip to Russia in the 1890s. Experience the thrill of being a suspected cholera sufferer.

The law says that if you have cholera all your belongings are taken away and you're imprisoned in a military barracks to stop the disease spreading.

1. Life in the barracks is very harsh and you don't get much food. But at least it's cheap and cheerful.

2 If you try to escape you'll be whipped.

THINK I'LL COME BACK NEXT YEAR

YOU'LL STILL BE HERE, NEXT YEAR

No wonder a traditional Russian curse said "May you get cholera." You can try this one out on the school bully ... if you dare.

Could you be a doctor?

YOU are famous Victorian physician John Snow (1813-1858). You're well known for pioneering the use of the painkiller chloroform in operations and now you're interested in cholera.

In 1854 cholera breaks out in London. Thousands die, including 700 in one small corner of Soho. The people here live in slums and 54 people share an outside toilet. (How do they all fit in?)

The toilet is oozing its disgusting contents into the drinking water of the nearby pump. All the cholera victims have drunk the water. You believe that the germs that caused cholera got into the water from the toilet.

1 What do you do?

a) Take away the toilet for testing.

b) Take some water from the pump for testing.

c) Take away the pump for testing.

245

2 Your tests show that there are germs in the water. What do you do next?

a) Drink the water to see if you get cholera.

b) Give the water to an enemy to see if they get cholera.

c) Take the handle off the pump so no one can use it.

Answers: 1 b) When people with cholera used the toilet the germs made their way into the drinking water. The disease was slow to develop because some sufferers used potties and emptied them out of the window. It was messy if diarrhoea landed on your head but at least it kept the germs out of the water supply.

AND THAT'S SUPPOSED TO MAKE ME FEEL BETTER?

2 c) The epidemic stopped. (It was ending anyway but the important thing was that it didn't flare up again.) Snow had proved the link between cholera and dirty water.

Of course, the world sat up and took notice and Snow became a national hero! *Didn't he?* Come off it: *Horrible Science* ain't no fairy tale! No one took any notice and when John Snow died aged 44, his discovery was forgotten. Forgotten, that is, until super-doc Robert Koch took an interest in cholera.

Koch-ya!

In 1883 cholera struck the Egyptian city of Alexandria but by the time Koch reached Egypt the cholera had all but disappeared. I bet he was gutted! Never one to miss out on research, he tried giving germs to crocodiles to see if they got cholera. If they had, they'd have shed crocodile tears!

Meanwhile Louis Pasteur had sent two assistants, Emile Roux and Louis Thuillier, to Alexandria to find the cholera germ. Unfortunately, they tried to grow germs in a broth rather than on a plate of jelly and this made it hard to sort out the many different types of germs in the broth. The two scientists became confused but Thellier still managed to catch cholera and die. Science can be tough sometimes.

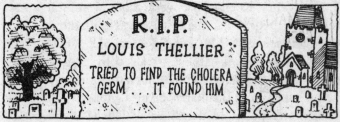

Koch went to East Africa and then to Calcutta, India, in search of cholera. In Calcutta he found thousands of people suffering from the disease. Naturally, he was delighted.

He cut open ten dead bodies and tested their festering diarrhoea and vomit and local water. He found vibrio germs in all of them, proving beyond doubt that the bacteria caused cholera.

Scientific note:
Actually, Italian scientist Fillipo Pacini described finding the cholera germ in the guts of victims as early as 1854 – but no one realized that the germ actually caused the disease and Pacini's discovery was forgotten.

WARNING! REALLY REVOLTING FACTS AHEAD.

Two really revolting cholera stories
1 Even after Koch's discovery there were some who refused to believe that the disease was caused by a germ. German scientist Max von Pettenkofer (1818-1901) thought that the disease was caused by chemicals. To prove his theory he actually *drank* a revolting mixture of germs taken from the diarrhoea of a cholera victim. Von Pettenkofer got mild diarrhoea which he claimed was nothing to do with the cholera. Yeah, right.

NOT BAD, PERHAPS A LITTLE MORE PEPPER

2 Actually this experience was not unique. A nurse told John Snow how one night she was tired after a long day nursing cholera patients and she felt like a drink. She was exhausted and dazed and picked up a large cup of tea and gulped it down. Only then did she realize that it wasn't a cup of tea she was drinking ... it was a potty full of diarrhoea! Amazingly, the nurse survived.

CUP OF TEA, DOCTOR?

But hold on – why didn't Max and the nurse get cholera? Well, they were being protected by their stomachs. Yes, the human stomach makes a strong acid that dissolves most of the cholera germs. Wanna know more?

Dare you discover (1) ... how stomach acid protects guts?

What you need:
Three glasses or jars
Yeast (the dried variety is fine)
Vinegar
Baking powder
Sugar
Three teaspoons

What you do:
1 Label the three glasses A, B and C.
2 Fill each with warm water and add three tablespoonfuls

of vinegar to B and C. Then add a heaped teaspoonful of baking powder to C and stir well until most of the froth has gone.

3 Add a teaspoonful of yeast and a heaped teaspoonful of sugar to each jar. Stir well.
4 Place the glasses in a warm place for an hour.

What do you notice?
a) Each glass contains milky beige-coloured liquid, and if I put my ear to the glasses I can hear a fizzing noise.

b) A and C are like this but not B.
c) Only B is like this, A and C are a disgusting shade of green.

Answer: b) In A and C the yeast is multiplying like cholera germs and the fizzing is carbon dioxide gas that is given off as the yeasts feed. The acid vinegar in B has killed most of the yeast and the sample is now a vile green colour. The acid in C was weakened by the baking powder. When your stomach acid is weak, perhaps because you've drunk lots of water, cholera germs survive to wreak havoc in the guts. Sickening – eh?

Dare you discover (2) ... how to make cholera cures?

If you get cholera you're going be very interested in finding a cure. Here are two possibilities...

Cure A

What you need:

A tea bag
Some mustard
A mug
A teaspoon

What you do:

1 Fill the mug with boiling water. (Grab an adult and ask them to help.)
2 Dunk the tea bag quickly in the water.
3 Add a level teaspoon of mustard and stir well.
4 Allow five minutes to cool and try a sip. (OK, you can sniff it instead!)
Note: if you don't like it you could always add milk and give it to the adult saying:

Cure B

What you need:

A mug
Some sugar
Some salt

What you do:

1 Fill the mug with boiling water. (Apologize to adult for the horrible trick you played and ask for help.)

2 Add a heaped teaspoonful of sugar and a quarter level teaspoon of salt and stir well.

3 Allow five minutes to cool, and then taste.

Which cure do you think works best?

a) A

b) B

c) They're equally useful but work in different ways.

Answer: b) Cure **A** is a traditional Spanish remedy and, like many old remedies, it's useless. Cure **B** is based on a mixture invented in Dacca, Bangladesh and Calcutta in the 1960s. It's designed to replace lost sugars and salts in the body and the boiling kills cholera germs in the water. This treatment has saved thousands of lives – it reverses the drying out so that the patient's white blood cells can kill off the cholera germs.

Today, cholera is still going strong in many parts of the world. Every so often the disease goes on a world tour, spread by ships that take polluted water into their ballast tanks (tanks of water that are used to stop the ship rolling in the sea) and released elsewhere. So although the disease can be cured, it's still a force to be reckoned with.

Mind you, if you think this sounds bad, in the next chapter you'll meet a whole new gang of disease-causers. They're a gang that cause really deadly diseases so you're sure to find them sickening.

Better put on that spacesuit...

ATISHOO!

VICIOUS VIRUSES

Your granny is wrong – small parcels don't always mean nice things. This chapter is about viruses – tiny things, far smaller even than bacteria. These tiny objects can ruin your life *for ever*. Fancy a closer look? Well, you'll *need* to look closer – a lot, lot closer.

Here they are...

A virus is basically a chemical called DNA (or, if you want to be teacher's pet, deoxyribose nucleic acid) surrounded by another chemical called a protein. DNA, as its long name suggests, is an incredibly complicated substance.

COULD I HAVE MORE INFORMATION ON THE STRUCTURE OF DEOXYRIBOSE NUCLEIC ACID, SIR?

TEACHER'S PET

It's found in all living cells and contains millions of chemical codes that control the cell's chemistry and affect how it grows and develops. Remember that viruses hijack the cells in your body and use them to make more viruses (see pages 167-168, if you've forgotten). Well, now for the deadly details...

Deadly disease fact file

NAME: Viruses

THE BASIC FACTS ABOUT WHAT THEY DO:

1 They sneak into the body through a cut or get in through the mouth or nose.

SNEAK!

2 They land on a cell and lock on to it using their protein outer coats.

VIRUS *LAND!*

CELL

SQUEEZE!

3 They squeeze their DNA through the cell wall or creep in with other chemicals that are being taken into the cell.

Copy! Copy! Copy! Copy!

4 They make for the nucleus where the cell's DNA is stored and activate the DNA chemically to program the cell to make lots more viruses. (This takes about half an hour.)

DEADLY DETAILS:

1 When the cell runs out of juice it dies and the viruses seek another victim!

SEEK! SEEK!

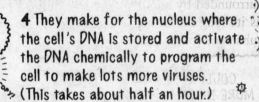

2 There are five million red blood cells in one drop of blood and each can hold 1,000 viruses – so there's plenty of room!

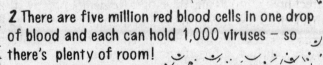

Vicious virus facts

1 One of the body's few defences is to kill the cells that viruses infect. Unfortunately this can sometimes make things worse. The Hepatitis B virus hides inside liver cells. The immune system kills the liver cells but you need your liver to live and sometimes the body ends up killing itself! That's dead unlucky.

2 There are actually viruses called bacteriophages (back-teer-rio-fay-ges) that attack bacteria. Doesn't your heart just bleed for the little darlings?

3 When viruses copy their DNA inside a human cell they often make mistakes – known as mutations (mu-tay-shuns). Whilst some of these mistakes can harm a virus others can make it better at infecting you. For example, they make chemical changes in the outer coat that disguise the virus so that the body's defences don't spot it. Sneaky, eh? As a result, it's hard for scientists to devise vaccines for diseases caused by these viruses ... diseases like flu.

Foul flu

Have you had flu? Sorry, silly question...

Flu is short for "influenza", which actually comes from the word "influence" and reflects an old belief that flu was caused by the influence of the stars. Well, you can thank your lucky stars if you don't get it...

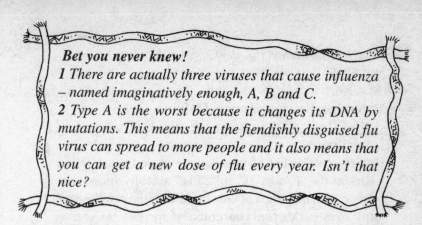

Like a cold, flu is spread by coughing or sneezing droplets of spit – oh, so you knew all about that? Well, did you know that you can even spread colds and flu by *talking*?

Dare you discover ... how speaking spreads flu?
What you need:
Yourself
A good supply of spit (drink a glass of water first)
A mirror

What you do:
1 Press your nose against the mirror.
2 Say the word "SPIT" loudly.
3 Say "DRY" loudly.

Which letters leave the most spit on the mirror?

a) "SPIT"

b) "DRY"

c) Neither, I never spit when I talk!

Answer:

a) The movement of your tongue as you speak letters such as the "P" and "T" in "SPIT" actually sprays spit. Of course, the drops of spit could be hiding millions of flu viruses. Maybe you could share this interesting information with a teacher who sprays spit as they talk. Or maybe not...

Teacher's tea-break teaser

Feeling cruel? Oh good. Well, wait until your teacher gets the flu and when she drags herself into school (most teachers seem to think it's a shame if you got sent home because there's no one to teach you) hammer on the staffroom door. Smile sweetly at your suffering school teacher and ask...

THE DAILY GLOBE

31 December 1918

FATAL FLU FEAR!

This year everyone has been talking about the worldwide flu epidemic. In the USA it's said that 500,000 have died, in the UK 200,000 and in India perhaps 20 million. It's even worse than the Black Death!

Dead bodies

THE FLU CAN KILL IN 48 HOURS! In India trains have been reported full of dead passengers and in some cities the streets are full of dead bodies. Here in America many cities have banned meetings in a bid to stop the disease spreading. Cinemas have shut down and churches are closed (except for funerals).

Bodies are buried standing up to save space.

PUBLIC HEALTH ADVERT

- Have you got the flu?

- Do YOU have a fever, headache, cough, has your skin turned blue or purple, are you coughing up blood? Looks like you've got the flu. Well, that's tough.

- *Don't* go out ... please!

- And *definitely* don't go near us!

- *Do* phone a funeral director – they're getting rather booked up just now.

FEVER

BLUE OR PURPLE SKIN

COUGHING UP BLOOD

Doctors' advice

We asked 20 different doctors for advice and received 21 different suggestions including ... drink coffee, take painkillers, drink alcohol, drink small doses of poison such as arsenic, eat potatoes, breathe wood-smoke, and pull your teeth and tonsils out (that'll help clear your throat).

☠ HORRIBLE HEALTH WARNING!

All these remedies were tried and they were all USELESS, so next time your little brother/sister gets flu, DON'T pull their teeth out or anything. Otherwise you'll end up in an unhealthy situation.

Bet you never knew!

1 The flu has been so deadly because it weakens the victims so much that bacteria can attack their lungs and cause the disease known as pneumonia. This results in fever, and difficulty breathing as the lungs fill with pus. Pneumonia can kill but nowadays it can be cured with antibiotics.

2 In the 1950s, American scientist Johan Hultin decided to find some of the 1918 virus. He went to a town in Alaska where the bodies of flu victims had been buried deep in the frozen ground. He dug up several preserved bodies and removed their lungs and tried to infect a ferret with the virus.

GLAD WE WEREN'T AROUND IN 1918 WITH THAT NASTY VIRUS

Unfortunately, it turned out to be dead. (That's the virus not the ferret – the ferret was no doubt relieved.)

3 After his retirement, Hultin returned to the village and dug up some more bodies. This time a team of US scientists led by Jeffrey Taubenberger studied the DNA of the virus and concluded that it came from pigs and then spread to people. It sounds a really horrible way to make a pig of yourself.

Teacher's tea-break teaser

Still feeling cruel? Yippee, cos today, having shaken off her flu, your teacher's gone down with a cold! That's tragic! Once again she's dragged herself off her sick bed to come and teach you lot. Hammer boldly on the staffroom door. Your teacher will appear, clutching a dripping hankie. Smile sweetly and ask:

Answer: Originally, perhaps – and that's neigh kidding! Scientists have discovered that one type of cold virus is similar to a virus that affects horses. They believe that humans caught the disease thousands of years ago from their trusty steeds. Perhaps that's why your teacher's a little hoarse?

A very small discovery

You might be wondering how scientists managed to discover viruses when they're so tiny. Well, the answer is that scientists didn't see viruses until 1930 when the electron microscope was invented. This brilliant bit of kit uses a beam of tiny blips of energy called electrons to show up tiny objects such as viruses. Sometimes it pays to think small! Before then scientists like Louis Pasteur realized that there was something causing viral diseases and they knew that it was very small because it went through the finest filters.

There was one particular virus called rabies that Pasteur struggled to make a vaccine for. It was a battle that was to have a dramatic and shocking conclusion...

Deadly disease fact file

NAME: Rabies

THE BASIC FACTS: Rabies is a virus that attacks animals such as dogs, foxes, bats, squirrels ... and humans. The disease drives the animals crazy – the dogs become mad, the bats go batty and the squirrels turn a bit nutty.

WOOF GRRR! FLAP GRRR! SQUEAK GRRR!

DEADLY DETAILS:

1 The virus heads for the brain where it blocks the nerve signals that cause swallowing. Swallowing becomes incredibly painful. Spit full of viruses dribbles out of the mouth.

2 Other symptoms are a terror of water (because the victim fears drinking because of the pain of swallowing) and violent fever.

3 Luckily, the virus is slow-moving and there's time to inject a vaccine and antitoxins to defeat the virus before it reaches the brain.

A matter of life or death

Paris, 1937

It was late afternoon when the young American woman arrived at the gates of the Pasteur Institute. There was no one about except an old man sweeping the yard.

"Good afternoon, Mademoiselle," he said politely. "Can I help you?"

"Oh no," she said. "I merely came to see..."

"Oui," said the old man proudly. "We get many visitors like yourself, but there is no one around now." He was a thin old man with a flat cap and grey stubble on his chin.

Just then there was a rumble of thunder and it began to rain heavily.

"Oh no!" exclaimed the young woman looking crossly at the sky.

The old man shrugged. "It is impossible! I cannot work with this rain. Mademoiselle, may I offer you a cup of coffee?"

"Why yes, thank you," she smiled.

The old man led the way to a cramped room, part caretaker's shed and part storeroom of dusty laboratory supplies.

"You are interested in the great Louis Pasteur perhaps?"

"Well, I'm training to be a teacher and next semester we're doing a project on him."

The old man beamed, his eyes were misty with pleasure.

"Ah, but that is wonderful. I remember Monsieur Pasteur well."

"No kidding – you knew *the* Louis Pasteur!" said the woman in amazement.

"Oui. Perhaps you would like to hear a story about Monsieur Pasteur?"

And as he busied himself with making the coffee, the old man launched into his tale.

"It was in 1884 that Pasteur was studying the disease rabies. You are familiar with this disease?"

The young woman shuddered and nodded.

"Well, Pasteur was experimenting with a vaccine made from rabbits. Rabbits that died of rabies. Pasteur dried their backbones that were, of course, full of the virus. He did this to weaken the virus and then he could inject it into dogs and, voilá, the dogs were protected from the rabies."

"One day a young woman knocked at his laboratory door. She had her son with her – boy named Joseph Meistner who two days before had been savaged by a rabid dog."

"A *rabid dog*! Hey – that's terrible. Was the kid in a bad way?"

The old man took his time answering, carefully pouring the coffee into two cracked mugs.

"The boy had been bitten on his hands, on his legs – everywhere! He was not expected to live. Pasteur knew that he had to try the vaccine on the boy or he would die.

"I remember the scene like it was yesterday. It was evening, the blinds were drawn in the laboratory, and there was a smell of chemicals. Pasteur was there in his velvet cap, offering advice as a doctor injected the boy with vaccine. Injected! Pah – it was more like being stabbed in the belly! Of course the boy was scared, very, very scared. But he was brave and did not cry out."

The old man stirred his coffee.

"And after the injection all anyone could do was wait. Wait and wait to see whether the injection would work. Wait to see if the boy would live ... or die."

There was a long silence broken only by a rumble of thunder.

"And did the boy die?" asked the woman anxiously.

"No – he did not. In fact, he is alive and well! Mademoiselle, I shall pretend no longer – the boy in the story was me. My name is Joseph Meistner!" The old man's voice shook. "Louis Pasteur saved my life. That night I promised myself that I would serve Pasteur in any way I could. And I have worked here all my life – so you see, I kept my word."

His voice was stronger now and full of pride. And the face of the old man who was Joseph Meistner wrinkled into a smile as he slowly sipped his coffee.

More vicious viruses

Viruses come in all shapes and sizes (though they are all fairly tiny). Here are two that you might have come across, and as usual Dr Grimgrave has all the bad news...

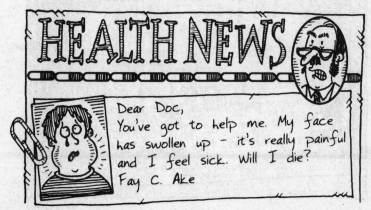

HEALTH NEWS

Dear Doc,
You've got to help me. My face has swollen up – it's really painful and I feel sick. Will I die?
Fay C. Ake

Dear Ms Ake,
You're suffering from the viral disease —
mumps. It's caused by a virus that
infects the spit-making glands on the
sides of your face. It gets
better on its own so go to bed
and take painkillers or keep
the area warm. Until then
you've just got to face it.
Dr Grimgrave

SWOLLEN
GLANDS

Dear Doc,
Thanks for your advice. I rested for two
weeks and I feel a lot better — my
appetite is back and I'm eating like a horse!
Fay C. Ake

Dear Ms Ake,
Eating like a horse are
you? Well, you'll only
get indigestion if you
don't sit down and use
a knife and fork like
everybody else.
Dr Grimgrave

Dear Doc,
I'm feeling sick and
achy and feverish
and my back and
chest and forehead are covered
in itching pus-filled spots.
I. B. Spottie
PS Sorry about the stains on
this letter.

> Dear Mr Spottie,
> You have chicken pox. It's a common virus and easy for an experienced doctor like me to spot. The best thing to do is rest and wait for the spots to become scabs and dry out. Don't bring them to me – I already have some in my collection. And don't pick them or they'll scar. At least you won't get chicken pox again, because your body will be immune to the virus.
> Goodbye!

Don't pick them!

Mind you, in the next chapter there's a virus so vicious and so nasty it'll make you *long* for chicken pox. Are you brave enough to read on ... or are you about to turn chicken?

CLUCK! CLUCK!

YELLOW DEATH

There are over 150 names for yellow fever and some of them aren't very nice. For instance, you could call it "yellow breeze" or "yellow jack" or (just so long as it isn't a mealtime) "black vomit".

Bet you never knew!

In Jamaica in 1740 Dr John Williams announced yellow fever was different to blackwater fever. This is a fever (surprise, surprise) in which your pee turns brown or red (but not usually black). Local doctor Parker Bennett disagreed and challenged Williams to a duel. In the fight both doctors were killed.

SCIENTIFIC NOTE

Williams was dead, but he was dead right. Blackwater fever is actually caused by another disease, malaria, attacking the kidneys (see page 296). The pee gets its colour from blood. Mind you, yellow fever is even worse! Would you care for a dose? Could it be worth it to get off school? ...

Sickening sick note 3: yellow fever

Dear teacher,

I'm so worried about ~~me~~ ....
~~I'm~~ s/he's bright yellow! First s/he
had a flushed face, fever and aching.
And now the poor dear is in terrible
pain and bringing up black vomit and
bleeding from the ears and nose. The
doctor says it's yellow fever, and I'm
at the end of my tether - I'm so
scared! So please excuse ~~me~~ her/him
for not doing any homework.

Signed,

An extremely concerned parent

blood →

sick

Sickening sick note notes

1 The black colour is congealed blood.
2 The disease is spread by the aedes (a-ee-dez) mosquito.
We trapped one of the little villains and extracted a
confession...

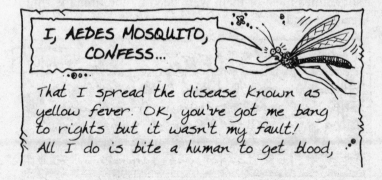

I, AEDES MOSQUITO,
CONFESS...

That I spread the disease known as
yellow fever. OK, you've got me bang
to rights but it wasn't my fault!
All I do is bite a human to get blood,

I mean, I'm a mosquito right - that's me job. I only take a drop and don't mean no harm. I'm usually around at dusk if anyone wants to donate blood. It's not my fault if the blood sometimes has the virus that causes yellow fever. I mean, how am I supposed to know? It's not as if the victim is bright yellow! Well, OK they are - but I'm hungry. So I bite another victim and they get sick. Well, that's sad. You're not going to squash me, are you? Are you?

If the yellow fever virus could be caught and put on trial for crimes against humanity here is what the charge sheet might have said.

Charges against the yellow fever virus
1 That on or about the seventeenth century you crossed the Atlantic from Africa inside mosquitoes in ships bound for America. That you infected the sailors so that sometimes most of them were dead by the time the ship reached land.

2 That once in South America you killed off millions of innocent monkeys that had no immunity to you.

3 That you caused deadly epidemics in the Americas, Caribbean and even parts of Europe. For example, in 1802 you killed 23,000 French troops in Haiti and in 1821 you killed one in six people in Barcelona, Spain.

4 You caused such terror that in the 1840s the people of Memphis, USA considered abandoning their fever-ridden city and burning it to the ground.

Daft doctors

1 As usual, the doctors were confused about yellow fever. To begin with they thought it was caused by – surprise, surprise – bad smells.

In the 1790s in Philadelphia, a city ravaged every year by the disease, Dr Benjamin Rush blamed rotting coffee beans in the docks. But this theory wasn't worth a bean.

2 A certain Dr Firth was so sure that the disease couldn't be caught like flu he actually *drank* the disgusting black vomit made by a sufferer and *injected* himself with the victim's blood. Although by rights he should have got the disease, it didn't actually develop – perhaps because the virus was weak. Still, don't try this at home.

But scientists were closing in on the yellow fever and in 1900 George M. Sternberg (of the US army) sent an élite team of scientists to Cuba to investigate the disease. Would they succeed when so many had failed? They were led by army doctor, Walter Reed. Here's what his reports to Sternberg might have looked like...

Four against the yellow death

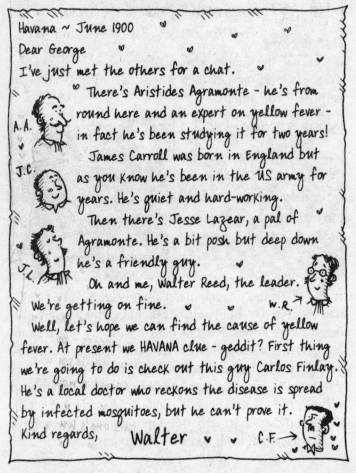

Havana ~ June 1900
Dear George
I've just met the others for a chat.

There's Aristides Agramonte - he's from round here and an expert on yellow fever - in fact he's been studying it for two years!

A.A.

James Carroll was born in England but as you know he's been in the US army for years. He's quiet and hard-working.

J.C.

Then there's Jesse Lazear, a pal of Agramonte. He's a bit posh but deep down he's a friendly guy.

J.L.

Oh and me, Walter Reed, the leader. We're getting on fine.

W.R.

Well, let's hope we can find the cause of yellow fever. At present we HAVANA clue - geddit? First thing we're going to do is check out this guy Carlos Finlay. He's a local doctor who reckons the disease is spread by infected mosquitoes, but he can't prove it.
Kind regards,   Walter   C.F.

July 1900

Dear George,

Strange things are happening at the army base. A soldier died of yellow fever whilst locked in the guard house. But the other prisoners didn't get the disease. Some soldiers have slept in the beds of yellow fever victims, complete with dried sick and poo on the sheets (soldiers ain't too fussy). But they didn't get the disease either! Blistering bedpans! Know what I'm thinking? I figure you can't get yellow fever by person-to-person - or even person-to-body-waste contact like an ordinary disease.

So maybe Finlay's right and it's something to do with them pesky mosquitoes? Jesse Lazear's been catching mosquitoes and letting them bite volunteers but so far no one has gone down with yellow fever - BLAST!

I'll keep you posted, Walter

September 1900

Dear George,

As you know I'm back in the States but I've kept in touch with the others and can report a success - sort of.

Carroll and Lazear were in the lab and Jesse was showing off how to get a mosquito to bite a person.

"Don't think this one's hungry," said Lazear.

275

"Maybe it'll take a bite of me?" said Carroll, and sure enough it did. Well, shiver my stethoscope! Blow me if Carroll's not got yellow fever!

Mind you, I shouldn't joke - he could die.

Well, we've got to try this experiment again. We've still got the mosquito and its little tummy is rumbling. Luckily, there's a very stupid soldier at the base called William Dean and he's volunteered to be bitten!

CHOMP!

Derrr

Five days later...
I've just heard Dean's got yellow fever! He says it must have been something he ate! That proves the mosquito spreads yellow fever. Success at last!

Walter

Deadly discoveries

1 The scientists had proved the mosquito spread yellow fever but fate was to play a cruel trick. A few days later Lazear was also bitten (quite by accident) and although Carroll and Dean survived the disease, Lazear did not. Sadly, he was not the only scientist to be killed by this deadly disease.

2 Japanese scientist Hideyo Noguchi (1876-1928) thought that yellow fever was caused by bacteria. He even made an antitoxin against the bacteria but of course it didn't work against yellow fever virus. In 1928 Hideyo was studying yellow fever in Africa when he died ... of yellow fever.

3 In 1927 Irish doctor Adrian Stokes (1887-1927) was in Africa trying to prove a link between yellow fever and monkeys when he caught the virus. He continued to experiment on monkeys using himself as a guinea pig, and proved that mosquitoes can pass the disease between monkeys and humans. Then he died.

4 Scientists didn't develop a vaccine to yellow fever until 1936. In that year a virus taken from a young African called Asibi was shown to be weakened so much that it no longer caused disease, but it made the body develop immunity. Since then the vaccine made from Asibi's virus has saved millions of lives.

Galloping Gorgas

Armed with the vital information that the aedes mosquito spreads yellow fever, scientists set about attacking the new enemy. None was more determined than US Major Walter Gorgas. With him it was all kind of *personal*.

When Gorgas had been a young officer his Colonel's daughter fell ill with yellow fever and the Colonel ordered Gorgas to speak at the girl's funeral. In fact, she recovered but Gorgas got the disease and the girl nursed him. They fell in love and got married.

In the 1880s a French attempt to build a canal across the Isthmus of Panama (the narrow bit between North and South America) failed when 52,816 labourers got yellow fever. In 1904 the Americans decided to have a go...

In 1904 Gorgas, by then a top army doctor, was ordered to Panama by the President to beat yellow fever. Gorgas sent thousands of men into the battle. He wanted oil poured on all open water so the mosquito couldn't lay eggs and bushes burnt so that the mosquito couldn't hide.

Gorgas had to face opposition from his bosses in the US Army.

Colonel Goethals complained:

By 1906 Panama was free of yellow fever and the canal was completed in 1913. For the first time ever, humans had taken on a deadly disease on its own ground ... and won!

Bet you never knew!
Today, yellow fever is still lurking in the tropics (the warm regions of the world) but it's no longer a massive killer. That's the good news – but one of its revolting relatives, dengue fever, is spreading. This disease is also spread by aedes mosquitoes and it's known as "breakbone fever" because it feels like all your bones and joints are breaking apart. Fancy a break off school, then?

Some good news at last...

It's typical. Just when we think we're beating a disease another one pops up. It's a bit worrying, isn't it? Well, here's a bit of good news. There's one deadly disease that we've beaten fair and square – for *ever*!

You'll find the next chapter a real shot in the arm...

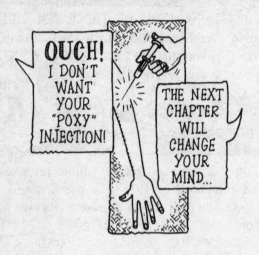

SMALLPOX SMASHED

For thousands of years a war has been raging between microbes and humans. It's a war without mercy on either side, and millions of humans and trillions of germs have died. In all this time once and only once have the humans ever won a decisive victory – over smallpox. But what was this disease like?

If you've ever had measles then you'll know what *that's* like. Can you imagine measles ONE HUNDRED times as bad? If not, you'd better read this...

Sickening sick notes 4: smallpox

Dear teacher,
I don't know what to do! The doctor says my poor .... has smallpox! It began with a violent raging fever and throwing up and agonizing muscle pains from head to toe and later a horrible rash. Now the fever is worse and the rash is a mass of huge pus-filled spots! Germs have attacked the spots and ~~my~~ his/her skin is rotting and falling off! I can't stand it and nor can poor .... Please excuse ~~me~~ him/her from all science lessons - *for ever!*
Signed,
Very worried parent

Sickening sick note notes

1 Like measles, smallpox is caused by a virus. The brick-shaped smallpox virus is called variola.

2 The virus can be spread by touching the scabs and by infected breath. If there was an outbreak of smallpox at your school they'd have to close down the whole school for months.

3 Unfortunately, I mean luckily, no one gets smallpox any more (for reasons you're about to discover) so your teacher might not believe your sick note and then she might realize that all the others were made up too.

This Is Your Death!

In its time smallpox killed millions of people. I wonder what the *This Is Your Death* people would make of it?

WELCOME TO THE TV PROGRAMME THAT PUTS THE LIFE BACK INTO DEATH.

Today we're at a high security laboratory to meet a celebrity who has touched the hearts of people around the world – and other parts of their bodies too. We've shrunk down to interview the smallpox virus – Variola major, this is your death!

THIS IS YOUR DEATH!

Wow! I don't get too many visitors here!

No one knows where you came from. But in your time you've been very close to royalty. Indeed, it's said you made a killing from your connections with them. Here are your royal chums... Come in Your Majesties!

I sure did.

GRRR!

Ramases V of Egypt (died 1157 BC), Mary II of England (died 1694), Peter II of Russia (died 1730) and Louis XV of France (died 1774).

Luis I of Spain (died 1742), two Emperors of Japan (both died 548) and the Inca Emperor Huayna-Capac (died 1526).

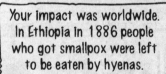

Er – nice to see you again guys.

Numerous people were left scarred by your scabs, including George Washington.

Yes, I've left my mark on history.

Your impact was worldwide. In Ethiopia in 1886 people who got smallpox were left to be eaten by hyenas.

GRRR!

I've always had a soft spot for animals!

Sinister smallpox stories

One of the first to study smallpox was Arab doctor, Abu Bakr Mohammed ibn Zakaria (860-932), known as al-Rhazes, who described the differences between smallpox and measles on the basis of observing the sufferers. Just in case you're wondering...

1 Measles makes you sneeze in the early stages and this gives you a red nose.

AS YOU CAN SEE, THIS MAN IS DELIGHTED THAT HE HASN'T GOT SMALLPOX

2 Measles spots are smaller than smallpox spots and don't form scabs.

3 With measles you also get white spots in the mouth.

Rhazes wrote 200 books, mostly about philosophy and religion – but his religious views fell foul of a powerful mullah (Islamic priest). The mullah ordered Rhazes to be beaten with his own book until either the book broke or his head broke.

CLONK!

OUCH! I WISH WE'D ONLY PRINTED PAPERBACKS

Unfortunately, Rhazes' head wasn't as thick as his book and he got brain damage and went blind.

Smallpox goes west

When smallpox arrived in America in 1521 it triggered the greatest disaster in human history, something that made the Black Death look like the Teddy Bear's Picnic. The disease was brought over by Europeans. Many Europeans had had the disease and their bodies were immune to it but the native Americans had never encountered smallpox (or other European diseases such as measles and flu) and so they had no protection.

And they had no more idea of how to cure the disease than the Europeans. The native treatment, sweating the disease out and then jumping into icy water, only hastened death. (Mind you, some schools still practise this technique – it's known as the "swimming lesson".)

For over 200 years smallpox happily rampaged through the Americas like a caterpillar in a cabbage patch. In all, one hundred *million* people may have died.

The defeat of smallpox began with a custom that developed separately in China and Turkey. It was called inoculation and it involved giving a person a mild dose of the disease to boost their immunity. It's a bit like vaccination, but this time the virus is alive. A remarkable woman worked to spread the custom around the world...

Hall of fame: Mary Wortley Montague (1689-1762) Nationality: British

Mary had every reason to hate smallpox. She was a beautiful and talented young woman of 26 when the disease struck. And it left horrific scars on her face. Before then her dad had tried to marry her off to an incredibly boring man named Clotworthy. (I didn't make that bit up, honest!) When Mary refused, her dad locked her in the house and got her sister to spy on her. (Little sisters can be vicious...)

Anyway, Mary escaped with her rich pompous boyfriend, Edward Montague, who became ambassador to Turkey.

And it was there that Mary came across inoculation. Here's what she might have written to her friend, Sarah Chiswell, in England...

Adrianople, 1717
Dear Sarah,
I've come across this wonderful method
for preventing smallpox! Every year an
old woman comes round asking if
anyone would like the smallpox cure.

If anyone's interested the old woman puts
some smallpox pus in a nutshell and puts this
on the end of a pin. Then she scratches their
skin and dabs a bit of pus into the
wound. In a few days each person falls
ill with a mild fever and spots and then
they get better and never get smallpox. Wow!
Of course, there's a down side. You've got a one
in four chance of getting full-blown smallpox,
and if you get it you'll probably die. But hey -
it's only a one in four chance and I can't wait
to try it out on my son and daughter.
Love,
    Mary

Mary's children survived. Back in England in 1718, Lady Mary suggested the treatment for the daughters of her friend the Princess of Wales. The Princess wasn't so sure so Mary suggested a horrifying experiment. Six criminals awaiting execution were given a deadly choice...

Would YOU be dying to take part? Anyway, the criminals survived (actually one had had smallpox and was immune anyway but he didn't let on) and the royal children were safely inoculated too. Mary became famous although not everyone liked her bossy manner. The poet Alexander Pope wrote some rude verses about her so she bought his book and used it to line her potty. And then she boasted that she plopped her poop on Pope.

Teacher's tea-break teaser

Important note: if you try this teaser and you get expelled you're on your own, OK.

Rap smartly on the staffroom door. When it squeaks open give your teacher a sunny smile and enquire:

Smallpox goes west (and this time for good)

In 1796, Jenner developed cowpox vaccinations to fight smallpox (remember that bit from page 209). So it was now possible to stop people getting smallpox. And unlike plague the disease didn't hide in wild animals and unlike yellow fever it wasn't spread by insects. The virus only lived in people and if everyone was vaccinated then the virus would die out. In 1966, following a suggestion by Russian scientists, the World Health Organization set out to do just that.

Led by US doctor Donald Henderson, 650 WHO health-workers scoured the world for smallpox. In Brazil a doctor was kidnapped but before he was released he insisted on vaccinating his captors against the disease.

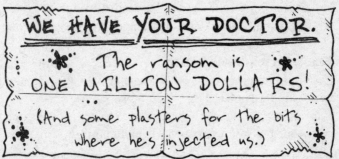

WE HAVE YOUR DOCTOR.

The ransom is ONE MILLION DOLLARS!

(And some plasters for the bits where he's injected us.)

Another doctor was killed by a native American arrow. Eventually the disease was found only in Somalia and Bangladesh and then in 1980 there came the long-awaited announcement. Smallpox had been wiped off the face of the Earth (though a few samples were kept for research). For the first time in millions of years humans had destroyed a deadly disease!

Well, that was the good news. But meanwhile new deadly diseases were appearing – but where were they coming from? And why did they have to be so *nasty*? Are they really out to get us? Read on and find out...

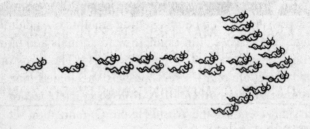

NASTY NEWCOMERS

I'm afraid the facts about some of these new diseases make rather miserable reading. Dr Grimgrave is happily putting together a dossier on some of the worst offenders...

☠ HORRIBLE HEALTH WARNING!

READERS MAY LIKE TO PUT A HANKIE OVER THEIR NOSE AND MOUTH AT THIS POINT. YOU DON'T WANT TO RISK CATCHING ANYTHING NASTY, DO YOU?

Rogue's Gallery

WANTED FOR MURDER

BACTERIAL DISEASES

LEGIONNAIRE'S DISEASE

First known appearance: Philadelphia, USA, 1976.

Known crimes: Killed former members of the American Legion staying at a hotel. Since then has appeared all over the world. I would

A NOTE FROM DR GRIMGRAVE
I object to the light-hearted presentation of serious factual information. Anyone would think that this book is a publication of a humorous nature.

like to study it further but
unfortunately none of my **patients**
has caught it.

Method of operation: Attacks the
lungs and causes fever.

Known associates: Lives
inside a protozoan that
lives in shower heads and
air conditioning systems.

Danger rating: Still rare
and can be treated with
antibiotics.

LYME DISEASE

First known appearance:
Studied by scientists at
Old Lyme, Connecticut,
USA 1975.

Known crimes: Attacked a group of
children in the town, they all
recovered. Since then has appeared
all over the USA and parts of
Europe, China, Japan and South Africa.

Method of operation: My colleague Dr
Gripe got this illness and it caused
him a few gripes I can tell you. He
suffered fever, rash, stiff neck,
aching joints and years of pain. But
luckily he was a patient patient.

Known associates: Lives
inside tiny biting bugs
such as deer ticks. The tick
collects the virus by biting
mice and can pass it on to
humans by biting them.

Tick

292

Danger rating: Not
fatal — can be treated
with antibiotics.

HUMOROUS NOTE
Teachers must be
a health hazard
because they're
always giving you
ticks. Sorry, Dr G!

VIRUSES

EBOLA

First known appearance:
Sudan and Congo
Republic, Africa, 1976.

Known crimes: Kills
between 50 and 80 per
cent of victims.

Method of operation:
Spread by contact
with body fluids
such as blood and
vomit. Symptoms
include violent
headaches, bleeding
from the ears,
eyeballs and bottom.
Hair and fingernails
drop off. Certainly
a fascinating
disease, I watched
a programme about
the symptoms whilst
eating supper last
night.

Known associates: None.

Danger rating: Very rare even in
Africa. All outbreaks have been
contained.

AIDS

First known appearance:
Africa, probably in the
1950s. There are actually
several varieties of the
HIV virus (Human Immuno-
deficiency Virus) that cause the
disease known as AIDS (Acquired
Immune Deficiency Syndrome).

Known crimes: If left untreated, kills
99.9 per cent of all its victims.

Method of operation:
1 Hides inside the DNA
of the T-cells where
it's impossible for
the immune system to
find it.

*Horribly complicated
– to get your head
round it you might
like to check back to
page 255.*

2 After several months or
even years, for unknown reasons, the
virus starts to attack more T-cells.

Basically what happens is that the
virus kills more and more T-cells
until the immune system can't fight
off germs such as TB bacteria.

Known associates: It is these other
diseases that then actually kill the
patient.

Danger rating: Deadly, but because
the virus is spread by contact with
body fluids such as blood, it's
quite hard to get. You can't get it
from someone coughing over you or
even from sharing a toothbrush or a
toilet with a sufferer, like some
idiots claim.

So why are we getting all these new diseases?

Ask two scientists and you'll be given three different answers (at least).

THE CLIMATE IS GETTING WARMER AND THIS MAKES IT EASIER FOR INSECTS THAT SPREAD DISEASE TO BREED.

AND AS PEOPLE TRAVEL MORE THEY TAKE GERMS WITH THEM. THIS MEANS THAT DISEASE CAN SPREAD FASTER.

AND DON'T FORGET MANY PEOPLE NOW LIVE CLOSE TOGETHER IN BIG CITIES WHERE DISEASES CAN SPREAD EASILY.

As usual with science there's no simple answer. But there's one explanation that many scientists support. Many of the new diseases are spread by animals. AIDS and ebola have been found in monkeys, Lyme disease is spread by ticks and so on. What seems to be happening is that as humans settle in wild areas of the world and cut down forests we pick up diseases that have existed there for thousands of years. That's probably how we first got the plague from the cute furry animals that normally carry it.

So it's all our fault? Charming!

Depressing reading, eh?

Well, cheer up – it gets worse. You know all those lovely diseases that we've been talking about and which you might have thought were beaten by modern medicine? Well, some old favourites have been crawling out of the dustbin of history. Take the lung disease TB...

TB: the bad news...

To cure TB you take antibiotics for up to a year. But most people feel better after a few months and the drugs are expensive so it's easy to give up the treatment. This is a massive mistake because it means that the remaining TB germs are the strongest and the most able to survive the drugs, and they can stage a comeback. In many parts of the world TB is now resistant to antibiotics. So today millions of children need to be tested for TB. (If you're a budding actor you could say "TB or not TB, that is the question.")

Malaria: more bad news

In Africa, 3,000 people die of malaria every day and it's getting worse. It's reckoned that a person gets bitten by an infected mosquito every *30 seconds*. (That person must be getting sick of it by now! Sorry, sick joke.)

In many parts of the world the mosquitoes that carry the disease can't be killed by sprays. The reason is the same as for the TB germs: the mosquitoes' bodies have learnt to deal with the poisons. And the protozoa that cause the disease are increasingly able to survive anti-malaria drugs.

Here's something to take your mind off it...

Could you be a doctor?
You're in Dr Grimgrave's waiting room. You've got a splinter in your little finger. (Let's hope he's in a good mood and doesn't cut it off!) The other patients aren't in the pink of health. Can you work out what's wrong with them...?

CLUE: Try looking back at the diseases mentioned in this book.

Some good news at long last!

Science *is* fighting back... Here's an exclusive peek at some of the latest high-tech drugs that are heading our way. Yes, here in one of Dr Grimgrave's medical magazines!

MEDICAL NEWS

NEW DRUG BREAKTHROUGHS!

Scientists are always working to develop new drugs. This week we report on the latest developments...

Amazing antibiotics

When bacteria have become resistant to an antibiotic scientists want to know why. It's usually because the

RESISTANT BACTERIA

ANTIBIOTIC PROBLEMS

bacteria make a chemical that sticks to the antibiotic and stops it working. As one drug company representative said: "It's a real sticky problem." One response is to add a chemical to the antibiotic that sticks to the bacteria chemical and stops *it* working.

298

Designer DNA

Scientists are trying to attack the DNA in a virus.

That's the chemical that controls how the virus develops (some viruses use a simpler chemical called RNA but the effect is the same).

The idea is to make a protein chemical that can stick to the DNA and stop it working. This stops the virus from multiplying.

Argh! My DNA's stopped working!

WANTED FOR MEDICAL COLLECTION

Dead body parts showing signs of unusual disease. Rare pustules, blisters and sores particularly welcome.
Contact:
Dr Grimgrave,
The Surgery,
Much Moaning.

BRAND NEW BREAKTHROUGHS!

Thanks to genetic engineering we can make bacteria produce large amounts of vital chemicals such as antitoxins or interferon. (As all readers know, interferon is the vital substance that stops viruses multiplying.) Another area of research is artificial antibodies called monoclonal antibodies. Grown in cells kept in laboratories, these chemicals can be used like antibodies to block toxins.

My monoclonal antibodies are growing well, this year

Next week

▷ Would we doctors be happier without patients?

▷ Fascinating gory operations in full colour.

▷ Our "long-running" series on body fluids features an in-depth report on diarrhoea and vomit.

WARNING!

The next bit won't just scare the socks off you – it might scare your toe nails off too!

Bet you never knew!

In 1997 something TERRIFYING happened. Scientists in Hong Kong found a new type of flu that attacked chickens. The virus that caused the flu was similar to the one that killed all those people in 1918. In just a few months, say the experts, the virus could have changed its DNA so that it could attack people. It could have swept round the world carried inside passengers on jet planes. And it might have killed hundreds of millions of people.

As things turned out, it didn't.

The scientists killed all the chickens that carried the disease and stopped it spreading. This time.

But will the next time be the *last time*? Perhaps, lurking somewhere out there is a germ so nasty, so vicious that it could wipe out life on this planet! Better read on and find out!

EPILOGUE: A SICKENING FUTURE?

So will a new disease appear and wipe us out?

The answer's no so please DON'T PANIC!

Even if there were such a disease (and some diseases are pretty anti-social as you've just found out), it's *not* going to destroy us and here's why. Doctors now have the knowledge and the technology to keep people healthier than they've ever been before.

> YOU'RE LATE FOR YOUR CHECKUP, MRS WHEELER!

> SORRY DOC, MY MOUNTAIN BIKE GOT A PUNCTURE COMING DOWN CRAGGY FELL

You can shiver at deadly diseases but you don't have to be scared of them. Most can be cured if treated quickly.

So even if a new deadly disease appears we know enough about diseases to ensure that it won't keep spreading. We know about techniques such as vaccination and antibiotics that can fight it. The truth is that although the battle against deadly diseases hasn't been won altogether – we're still gaining ground.

And there's more. For a disease to wipe us out it would have to kill us before scientists could devise any kind of treatment. Of course a few diseases *do* kill quickly – think of the 1918 influenza. But most diseases aren't that rapid – for a horribly good reason. If people died in five minutes then the germs would be buried with their first victim and never spread. And being buried alive is a nasty fate – even for a germ.

But if the disease spreads over a period of months and years then there would be time for some people to come into contact with just a few germs and get a mild dose of the disease. These people would fall ill and recover and so develop immunity.

And there's an even better reason why we should be OK. *Human nature.*

This has been a book about death and suffering and pain. But in the worst times you can sometimes glimpse the best in people. People like the scientists who risk their lives and sometimes die to conquer a particular deadly disease. Or the volunteers who agree to take part in experiments that might leave them sick or dying.

Or the doctors who work round the clock to keep their patients alive, or George Kasson who raced to save children from diphtheria.

Ultimately, people try to help one another. It's the best way for us all to survive, and it's the reason why, whatever happens, humans will continue to fight and win the battle against deadly diseases. And that's the not-so-horrible truth!